College Education
and the Campus Revolution

College Education
and the
Campus Revolution

by
John E. Cantelon

THE WESTMINSTER PRESS
Philadelphia

STANDARD BOOK NO. 664-24863-2
LIBRARY OF CONGRESS CATALOG CARD NO. 73-83132

PUBLISHED BY THE WESTMINSTER PRESS ®
PHILADELPHIA, PENNSYLVANIA

PRINTED IN THE UNITED STATES OF AMERICA

To
Joy, Barbara, and Charles
whose love and loyalty revolutionized my life
and helped me grow

Preface

N EXT TO THE FAMILY, the college is the most threatened and problematic institution in modern American
society. There is an increasing amount of uncertainty about
both the goals and the methods of higher education. Where
until recently it would have been ludicrous to ask whether
the liberal arts college has a viable future, today it is not.

Literally hundreds of volumes and thousands of surveys
have appeared analyzing and criticizing every facet of
college life. It is with some hesitancy that one adds to this
already formidable accumulation of material. But there is
a need to examine some of the fundamental questions that
appear to be emerging from this welter of research and
analysis and to propose some answers to them for the
consideration of those interested in the present state and
possible future of higher education. There is, in educational
circles, much discussion of the role of the generalist as
over against the specialist in the modern American university. One of the functions of the generalist is to summarize
and make as clear as possible in nontechnical language
what he regards to be the basic issues and insights dis-
cerned by the creative thinkers of an era. If he is competent,
he can state with some lucidity what these analyses may
mean for our common social life and for the major institutions of our society. The present work is the product of a
generalist dedicated to these ends. Because there is so
much literature in the field and so little time to read it all,
it would appear only fair to begin by stating the focus of
this work and the perspective of the author so that the
reader may judge whether the areas to be explored are of
interest to him.

The author would identify himself as a Christian human-ist the perimeters of whose doctrinal orthodoxy have been shattered and blurred by the impact of radical religious, psychological, political, and social theories, and fifteen years of varied experience in the field of higher education. Paul Tillich's system, which he hoped might have some relevance for at least a decade, still proves helpful in pro-viding a viable perspective if not a total pattern for making sense out of an increasingly secular age. But the overall outlook is most eclectic, reflecting an era in which the breakdown of world views has had the result of making one feel closer to reality with its promises as well as its threats.

The general pattern of the book is as follows: First, the background of our so-called revolutionary era is explored and the problem raised as to whether it is really revolution-ary enough or whether the destructiveness of revolution does not arise, in part at least, because it has been restricted in far too narrow a field. Secondly, the specific focus of concern is the liberal arts college, particularly the college within the major universities. It is argued that it is in the colleges that the great issues of the future of our society are being decided. Thirdly, particular concern is centered on the role of the humanities within the curriculum of the liberal arts college, especially the issue of their relationship to the sciences in the overall problem of keeping human life human. Fourthly, attention is given to the attitudes of the activist student generation and how the structures and curricula of the college may contribute to making creative the revolutionary atmosphere that characterizes many campuses. Finally, some rather immodest proposals are set forth with respect to experimentation in liberal arts edu-cation.

J. E. C.

University of Southern California

Contents

Contents

1

Rapid Change in Education: How Many R.P.M.'s?

I T IS MORE than a commonplace to observe that in virtually every area of human life we are living in the most revolutionary era in human experience. Indeed, it is one of the most significant factors of the contemporary revolution that changes are occurring simultaneously in all facets of human life. The massive scope if not the inclusive breadth of change may be seen in the tortuous reactions taking place in all the major institutions of society. Government and health services, civil law and business structures, mass communication and modes of transportation, all show the impact of that great force that has transformed the modern world—technology. Any number of pervasive social causes might be identified as contributing to this rapid change—the legacy of political upheaval wrought by two world wars—the awakening of the so-called developing nations—the agony of the struggle for social justice. But behind these, and undergirding every other force that is making for change, lies the knowledge explosion and the technology that has resulted from it. In an incredibly short period of time (graduate study was only begun in American universities at Johns Hopkins University in 1876) research, principally in the field of natural and social sciences, has brought into existence a new era.[1] The advent of technology has been as important a movement in human history as the transition from nomadic to agricultural life at the dawn of history or the movement from rural agricultural to urban industrial society in the nineteenth century. It appears likely that the impact of cybernation upon the technological revolution will bring about a third or, as it has been called, a triple revolution.[2] Coming so quickly upon the heels of the modern industrial change, this revolution tends to merge into it and produce the most massive change in human history. The question is raised as to whether the velocity and impact of the triple revolution will be such as to destroy human society altogether.

The primary and most evident impact of the contemporary knowledge explosion has been the transformation of the fabric of society brought about by technology. It may be argued that virtually every change now affecting society is due to the application of technology and its implications. To cite but one example, consider the impact of technology in the field of agriculture upon the racial revolution. Without new farming techniques complemented by the attraction of urban wartime jobs and accompanied by such technically induced problems as agricultural surplus, government price supports, acreage control, etc., there would not have been the mass migration of black men and women to the cities, North and South, where their presence in the ghettos challenged not only patterns of discrimination but the continued viability of urban life as well.

What the technological revolution—the fruit of the knowledge explosion—has meant to those who have benefited from it and those who have not but are no longer ignorant of its benefits—is a change in the fundamental quality of human life. It is not merely the final demise of the medieval conception of human life as nasty, brutish, and short—although that certainly is a factor among the have-nots of the world whose lives are still being led in a feudal type of society; it has also entailed a dawning awareness that the full human potential has scarcely been recognized. Millions now believe that a marginal existence in a "scarcity economy" has no more necessity about it than the continuance of serfdom in a modern state. The technological era has virtually solved the problem of production although it has not, as has been often observed, mastered the problems of distribution. At one time many people were convinced that the improved life of the bourgeois was either the result of the uncovenanted mercies of an arbitrary deity or the precarious outcome of implacable natural or economic laws such as the survival of the fittest or the rule of supply and demand. Those so convinced were and are naturally members of this favored class and they were and still are in control of the principal institutions of their societies. But this "scarcity minded" outlook is no longer convincing to the mass of deprived humanity and although many of them do not at present have control of the destiny of their lives or nations, they mean to have it as quickly as possible.

Among the dominant middle class in the Western societies there is the conviction for which convincing evidence is claimed that the veneer of civilization is extremely thin and its achievements precariously fragile. The argument is that order must be preserved. Thus any attempt to change the established way of things runs the danger of inviting chaos. We will have occasion to explore this conviction later, but it is sufficient at this point to note that these arguments for restraint and for continuation of the establishment have increasingly little force among the dispossessed in the American ghettos or in the developing nations around the world. The unfortunate result is, on the one hand, that many of the beneficiaries of the present establishment are becoming more reactionary than the facts of social health or a prudent concern for their own futures would dictate and that, on the other hand, the have-nots are becoming more desperate and violent in rejecting these claims than may be tolerable without general social disaster.

The quality of human life brought about by the technological revolution is characterized by continued great inequalities. But it must be understood as also constituting a new life-style. Indeed, the most important outcome of the technological era, generated by the knowledge explosion, has been the emergence of a life-style. One of the principal characteristics of this new life-style is its this-worldly orientation. Western man inherited from his dominant religious traditions a transcendent orientation. Existence on earth was regarded as a testing or preparatory experience for the eternal life in heaven. Long before Marx it had been noted that the focus on the next world had its definite advantage for those in control of this one. But in an era of economic scarcity it was certainly more convincing and necessary to provide some means of rationalizing inequitable distribution of meager resources. Today such a rationalization is no longer necessary nor is it possible.

Commentators on the present college generation have termed it the "now" generation—impatient, unwilling to postpone until tomorrow the possible pleasures of today. As in so many areas, the college generation typifies the ethos of the whole of humanity. In the transformation from a life-style transcendentally oriented to the imminence of a this-worldly life we find a change from the "sweet bye and bye" to the "now" time scale.

Reasons why many of the college students today are so sensitive in expressing cultural attitudes stem from several factors. First, college students reflect the increasingly high educational level of their parents; they come to college with a background of having been raised by an intelligentsia sensitive in the sense of being other-directed and success-ful. Secondly, this college generation has benefited from the educational enrichment that took place in American high schools after the launching of Sputnik. Thus, freshmen frequently find that their initial courses in college are less challenging and stimulating than some of their courses were in their senior year in high school. This better prep-aration in high school has made students more mature intellectually in college. Also it has been pointed out that luxury has some of the same impacts as extreme depriva-tion upon the outlook of those who experience it. Youth in the ghettos and in the suburbs both have experienced an

Oedipal upbringing without a father at home (although for different reasons). It has also been noted that extreme wealth has the same impact in removing motivation for social betterment as does extreme deprivation.[3]

There is a third matter, which will be noted later: the way in which this college generation, or a significant part of it, seems to be undergoing a kind of sensitization in preparation for the needs of a changed world. This may seem something of a vague and mystical judgment, but perhaps it is true that college students are responding to the needs of the next evolutionary stage in human development.

Another factor that is contributing to the revolutionary tenor of our era is the increased length in the span of human life. The increased length of life not only exacerbates the problems of birth and death rates, food production, employment, gerontology, etc., but it has meant that each person lives through a whole series of radical changes in his or her lifetime. Before the modern era, save for rare accident of birth, a person's three score years and ten would normally be lived out in the context of very slowly changing social milieu. Even changes that did occur or the dangers that loomed were within the bounds of what might be expected as normal, e.g., quarrels between kings, crop failures, etc. But since the advent of the technological revolution, the scope and speed of change have increased incredibly. Henry Adams' thesis of progressive acceleration has proven to be true, including the projection of something of a rocket-like acceleration in the last half of the twentieth century.

What this has meant is that change that previously would have been ingested by a number of generations now takes place not only once but several times in the life-span of a single individual. And the prolongation of human life due to the advancement in the field of medicine merely increases the number of these radical new experiences. Thus by the time students have entered college they are already "older" than any previous generation. They have lived a number of previous human lifetimes, and many of them have adapted to this kind of situation by becoming far more flexible and apparently less committed to the convictions of the past. Who, after all, knows what tomorrow may bring? Again it is the technological revolution that has had its impact and which has helped to bring about this revolution of accelerated and lengthened lifetimes.

The technology that has made possible the longer and potentially more abundant life has already produced immense but frequently unrecognized changes in the patterns of human growth and development. Adolescence itself is a by-product of the industrial age. Until the dawn of technology there was an almost imperceptible transition from childhood to adult responsibility. The child moved directly from his mother's knee to work on the farm or in the family craft shop. But the intricate machinery of the new complex technological era required that children undergo longer and longer periods of training before they were prepared to take upon themselves adult roles. It is this protracted adolescence which, Erik Erikson reminds us, precipitated in young adults the identity crisis with which we have become so familiar. This identity crisis has been increased in Western countries because of the tendency to establish identity by means of the work one performs. The answer to the question of who one is most frequently is given in terms of what one does. There has thus developed a most important separation between being and doing about which we will have more to say later.

Young people find this question of identity increasingly problematic as they are engaged in protracted education, only the latter stages of which are vocationally focused. This may be one of the reasons why the so-called "vocational" subculture within our colleges has been less rebellious than the so-called "academic" or "activist" subcultures. This may be so because the vocationally oriented have, to some extent, answered their identity problems while the other groups are still troubled by them. The vocational problem would seem to be one primarily affecting males in our society, despite the increase in the number of women who are seeking careers. But there is evidence to indicate that the identity crisis is faced in a rather specific way by married women. Studies show that what is referred to as the "two-family family" is being proposed as an answer to the identity problem on the part of some women. They raise a family while they are still young and after the first batch of children has gone, thanks to medical advances and the way in which family-planning is now possible, a second family may be arranged for. This presumably answers the problem of women's identity in later life, but it certainly raises problems in a world already suffering from an acute population explosion!

It is also important to recognize that, because of the technological advances, this generation of young people is among the first to know they are economic liabilities to their parents. Up to this time, children on the farm or in the craft shop were a definite economic advantage. They contributed to and had a sense of helping to maintain the family structure. Today children know that they are primarily an expense. When they are still called upon to perform tasks by parents who are imbued with the Protestant work ethic, such as yard-mowing or dishwasher-loading, they sense that what they perform is busywork. It is not extraordinary that these young people react in a way analogous to the energetic executive who is retired on a pension. All his physical needs are taken care of but he frequently loses his sense of the identity and worth which had come to him through the performance of his job. Many retired persons under such conditions go through periods of great mental turmoil. Something like this is the experience of the children of the affluent middle class, and when this happens to young people the identity crisis is further complicated by their lack of a past career to solace them, plus their possession of even more abundant energy. It is no wonder that a generation of "superannuated" young people displays characteristics of restlessness, protest, and rebellion.

But it is not merely the problem of the postponement of the taking-up of one specific identity-bestowing career. The knowledge explosion has further complicated this issue of identity by producing conditions in which not one but several careers may be likely for the well educated in our society. Studies show, for example, that persons trained as engineers frequently end up performing a number of different kinds of administrative jobs in their lifetimes. Because of the increased tendency toward specialization in the complex technological era, there is also pressure to change vocational focus in order to escape the boredom of a lifetime of concentration on a very narrow field of interest. And on top of all this must be added the confusion of educators who must admit that they face the dilemma of trying to train young people for vocations which, because of fast-changing technology, are either unknown or only dimly perceived at present.

This identity crisis of the young, the multiple careers for adults, and increasingly long periods of retirement for the elderly, all help to underscore the problem of the quality and meaning of human life as it is now and will be in the future. Thus these vocational and identity problems further the trend away from man's preoccupation with transcendent answers to the question of the meaning of human life and focus our attention increasingly on the immanent problems of today's and tomorrow's world. This shift was already given dramatic expression in the nineteenth century with Feuerbach's assertion that all theology is anthropology. But this shift of attention from God to man makes the problem all the more acute since our ideas of anthropology seem to be woefully inadequate to match the needs of our time. The nineteenth century raised the question of the survival of God, but for the twentieth century the question is the survival of man.

These technological developments and their attendant problems then serve to focus attention back on the fundamental question of the nature of man. Humanity, however it is conceived, is always an achievement, never something merely given. The task of the humanization of man has been one of the traditional roles of higher education. Particularly the college has been the setting for this most basic of all activities. And of all the disciplines within the college, the humanities have been those most traditionally charged with this task. But the humanities took their decisive form long before the dawn of the technological era, developing as they did out of the medieval trivium and quadrivium. Thus the identity problem of our era can scarcely be solved by any simple stress on a return to a study of the humane subject fields. The humanities have themselves been decisively modified and, one might say, severely damaged by the transition that has caused them to be replaced by the sciences as the dominant concern of higher education. While it is still possible to assert the importance of the liberating arts as the means of freeing men from ignorance, it is not at all clear what they liberate man for. Thus the problem remains as to what positive conceptions of humanity young people are being introduced to and encouraged to adopt.

The problem is not simply one of priority in distributing educational resources, although that is a real one. Actually, the humanities have done quite well in terms of expansion since the period of World War II.[4] The more pressing problem is the sense of loss of purpose and meaning among professors in the humane disciplines. In a product-oriented society scientists can demonstrate the results of their research and teaching in terms of tangible products. But as Prof. William Arrowsmith of the University of Texas has noted, professors in the humanities have tended to draw back from accepting their role as helping to create humane persons.[5] They have recoiled from the conception that their task includes being models of a certain kind of humane life and have taken refuge in efforts that are imitative of the scientists, e.g., studies involving quantification, statistical comparisons, etc. Thus the technological revolution has produced a major change in society, one that has received too little attention, that of the self-understanding, structure, and mood of the college itself—that place where the future leaders of society gain their conception of self-identity.

Further exploration will indicate that some of the principal dilemmas confronting higher education today illustrate the same dislocation occasioned by the technological revolution based, in turn, upon the knowledge explosion which itself is largely a product of higher education. Three of these major problems involve the curriculum, the issue of the governance of institutions of higher learning, and the relationship between institutions of higher learning and their communities.

One of the most vexing problems faced by the liberal arts college in the area of curriculum centers on the problem of General Education or those courses common to all students which provide the base from which specialization may move. This problem stems in part from the unequal pressure applied by the sciences, the acknowledged instigators of the technological revolution, and the humanities which are unable to make any analogous claim or to exert similar kinds of pressure. The need certainly is not to diminish the changes that flow from the technological revolution but to balance them by aiding and abetting an equivalently vital humane revolution.

Another major problem facing higher education centers on the issue of the governance of colleges and universities. The question is, Who does in fact control and who ought in theory to control colleges and universities and what should the scope of that control be? This raises the question of the function of boards of trustees, the administration, the faculty, and the whole area of *in loco parentis*—that is, How much of the student's life is the business of the college? This question of control must indeed be answered to some extent before the curriculum issue centering on General Education can be solved.

It has been noted before that the college and university have increasingly modeled themselves after the pattern of the dominant structure of our technological society—the business corporation. The corporation pattern has provided for more efficiency in the running of institutions of higher learning, but it has also had an unhealthy effect in terms of the relationship it has engendered between faculty and administration.[6] But there are also other areas in the general question of the governance of colleges which are significant and which betray the excessive influence of the technological revolution upon education. One is the departmental organization of the colleges and, secondly, the *in loco parentis* issue already mentioned.

There are two primary reasons that lay behind the parental roles which colleges once performed and which now are almost everywhere being repudiated or so modified as to be unrecognizable. The first was the conception of the college inherited from the ancient British universities with their residential requirements. Behind this form of education lay a conception that a college education was not merely acquiring facts or learning techniques but the development of a particular life-style characterized by the ability to be articulate about the whole range of culture. It presumed something which has largely been forgotten, that there was a definite connection between community and communication. The kind of truth that a college should be concerned about is best or even only discovered within a community. This increasingly vaguely understood British heritage was strengthened in the American frontier society by the necessity of civilizing the young men who went to college from the rough environment of the frontier. But American education has more recently been influenced by Continental patterns, in which the student's connection with his university was solely academic with no living requirements and little college discipline. It was however urbanization, the product of the technological era, which dealt the decisive blow to the attempt to control the total environment of student life. The swallowing up of campuses by expanding cities with the resulting personal anonymity, the automobile, freeways, the affluent life, birth control pills (all of these products of the technological era), have made the policing of student life impossible. On every side one hears educators surrender to what seems to be inevitable.

For example, Dr. Lewis B. Mayhew, professor of education at Stanford, argues that what a student does in his personal life is of no business to the college. Its sole concern, he says, should be the student's academic performance.[7]

There is obviously great disagreement between this strictly limited role which Dr. Mayhew argues that institutions of higher learning should play and our argument that, for better or worse, many of the functions formerly performed by family, church, and political structures do increasingly devolve upon the college and university. What is more, all evidence points to the fact that it is fallacious to attempt to separate the academic life from its total environment. From the Jacob report of 1957 to the present date, research indicates that the co-curriculum is even more important than the classroom curriculum in shaping student values. Unless one wishes to acquiesce to the position that a college education is merely the impartation of facts and some techniques, an educator cannot forgo concern about the full range of a student's personal experiences. This does not mean that, to use Dr. Mayhew's examples, students ought to be prevented from engaging in various forms of social action and protest. Indeed, our argument is that they must be encouraged by their institutions to have this kind of involvement. It must also be noted that there are few indications that these other (nonacademic) institutions, family and church, are in fact in a position, no matter how willing they may be, to take up this burden. One may agree with Dr. Mayhew that it might be desirable if they did. And one can appreciate that as an educator he would prefer that other structures were given this onerous task. But unless there is more evidence than appears at the moment to indicate that church, family, and political structures are in fact being renewed so as to permit them to resume former functions, the fact is that the college is the only institution left to do so. Colleges must be concerned about the co-curriculum just because it is more important in determining a student's values, attitudes, and motivations than anything that goes on within the formal classroom. Certainly many traditional regulations, e.g., hours for women but not for men, the question of alcohol in the dormitories, rules on clothing, are indefensible today, if they ever were. But it is curious that when all indicators are that more concern should be focused on every aspect of student life, many educators should capitulate and say that nothing can be done except concentrate upon what goes on in the classroom.

The answer to the problem posed by an outmoded *in loco parentis* role for institutions of higher learning may be found in a reorganization of the humanities, not in imposing new sets of revised regulations upon students. It may also be found in the way in which dormitory life is organized and the degree to which faculty-student relationships are encouraged. It is recognized that students must be represented in the decision-making process which relates to every aspect of campus life. Securing their participation in helping to determine the structures that affect the quality of their lives is an important dimension in the maturing process. There is, however, debate as to whether student representation should be on official university committees or whether students should set up parallel structures and committees. The former plan may provide for growth through observation but it also tends to neutralize significant student participation. Student members on committees tend to be overwhelmed and silent. The latter plan is much more risky, but it may be a risk that is necessary to take. The parallel may exist between separate student committees and the role of the developing Black Power groups as an essential stage in the struggle for racial justice.

The whole issue of problems posed by the question of university and college governance points to the fact that technological revolution and its by-products should not be the single determinant in shaping the institutions of our society. What is needed is not the securing of quiet, repressing revolution but more revolution in other areas of life to balance the impact of technologically produced change.

The departmental structure of colleges and universities has its origins in the quite ancient past and flows out of what has been termed the "clericalization of the disciplines." Neat-minded clerics drew the boundaries around academic disciplines, parceling them out among the several departments. Gradually these departments increased in power so that most of the important college functions take place within them—constructing curriculum, promotion, hiring of faculty, raising salaries, etc. One problem raised by the increased power within the particular departments is indicated by the reluctance of departments to support joint programs in the field of General Education. Another, perhaps more pressing problem, is of a similar nature. This problem arises out of the fact that the areas of study to which academicians are increasingly addressing themselves just do not yield to the type of organization presupposed in the departmental structures. The needs of the community and the interest of students are more "issue centered," i.e., they focus broadly on the host of problems raised by technology and the urban crisis. To deal adequately with these giant issues involves bringing together a large number of disciplines and the fact is that present departmental structures do not facilitate this kind of cooperation. Thus we frequently find students and administrators in agreement as to curriculum changes that would facilitate issue-centered education while the faculty, with their professional careers centered in their own departments, constitute openly or covertly opposition groups to such moves.

Another major problem in our colleges and universities, if imaginatively faced, may contain within itself some answers to the first two problems mentioned. This problem revolves around the issue of the relationship between academic institutions and their environments. Since World War II colleges and universities have increasingly served the needs of the nation as well as their local communities. Part of this increased service orientation was due to the important place that university research played in industrial and military activities. But also it represented the increased support that higher education gained from the community in general. Unlike older colleges, modern institutions of higher learning exist without walls between them and the community. Thus the traditional "town and gown warfare" is taking on entirely different forms and directions.

But the cooperation between college and community has forced to the forefront a major issue regarding the function of higher education in our society. The question is whether a college or university should be a center for independent study and criticism, standing in detachment from the community, or whether it should be a primary agency for social change within the community. This problem exists in many forms. It poses little difficulty if the community service is viewed as providing what the society feels it needs to operate its various institutions as they are and to staff the professions as they are currently functioning. If this is understood, there is little debate. The university and college is then regarded as an extension or training ground of the establishment. Only the scattered voices of a few educational traditionalists would insist upon a greater emphasis upon pure research and social criticism than is now the case in state and industrially supported institutions. But this issue is a very touchy one when it is phrased in another form, that is, whether the university should bring its critical expertise to bear upon the total reconstruction of society, including its institutions and particularly with respect to the urban crisis and the quality of human life.

Educators, such as Robert Hutchins, have questioned whether there is a single university in America that is functioning as an independent locus of criticism. Certainly most universities are understandably going to continue serving society in the sense of staffing and providing personnel and research for government and industry. But in addition to this task, and influencing how this task is performed, there needs to be added the cultivation of the critical role and the direct involvement of the campus in the primary social crises. This must be encouraged for reasons which, we trust, will become evident.

It is not a matter of settling for one of the functions of the university or the other—either detached criticism or involved social action. Both are necessary for the performance of the total responsibility of the university to its society. This raises the issue of whether it is at all possible to be detached and objective and at the same time involved. A most important problem revolves around this issue and will be examined in some detail, for it is an issue that has to do with the increasing demands students are making for immediate sensate experience. But, for the present, it is sufficient to note that the only kind of service that will change society involves the application of critical principles. It is not necessary to adopt all of the Marxist position held by Herbert Marcuse in order to agree with his point that the full use of man's reason always involves a dialectical process of criticism. The purpose of knowledge is not just to know things as they are but to change them.

One of the problems that must be faced in bringing the resources of higher education more closely into relationship with the problems of society is that faculty are frequently predisposed to remaining detached from social problems by virtue of the kind of mental outlook which led them into their vocation. The reason they made their choice of an academic profession was because they did not wish to become too much involved in the world. The ivory tower of the college may have seemed to them an ideal refuge from the madding crowd. Administrators, unlike many faculty, do not shy away from the hurly-burly of the world, but they tend to be reluctant to move their institutions too rapidly in the direction of social action because of the fear of losing financial support from private industry or from state legislatures.

Among the four student subcultures only the activist group is alive to the need of bringing the resources of the university directly to bear on the problems of society.[8] But there are other movements at work within the university which may overcome the predisposition of the various elements of the university community not to move in the direction of social involvement. Indications are evident in the trend toward setting up experimental colleges, urban semesters, ecological institutes, and various types of urban consortia. As such units develop, often without the conscious facing of the fundamental questions, institutions of higher learning find themselves increasingly, somewhat unconsciously, fulfilling the functions of social change agents. When this occurs and these units become regularized within the structure of college and university, there is the possibility that the resulting modifications may bring about a creative solution to the other two dilemmas already noted. The problem of General Education may be solved as General Education itself is restructured in relationship to an issue-oriented curriculum. The first two years of a curriculum may then consist of a pattern of study and involvement in some aspects of community life. A "great books" or "great ideas" oriented curriculum becomes more meaningful when it is related to the value conflicts of contemporary society. Moreover, patterns of cooperation among various disciplines, necessitated by urban semesters and ecological programs, begin to break down the artificiality of the old departmental lines. What is called the governance problem may also be helped by new cooperation among students, administrators, and faculty when they face not the niceties of political balances of power among themselves, but rather the needs of an increasingly demanding urban crisis. When the college is no longer looked upon as an enforcer of rules and regulations which support an outworn morality but can be considered as an institution through which faculty, administrators, and students together may engage in research and assistance to solve pressing problems of the community, then the issue of the co-curriculum will not be the problem that it is today. In this kind of education what happens outside the classroom is as important as classroom work and the two serve to supplement each other to the infinite improvement among other things of student motivation to learn.

We have looked at the general revolutionary background against which higher education is set today. We have seen how pervasive the revolutionary impact has been in all phases of human life, especially within the college and university. But, as we have noted, the enormous changes have all been the result of one particular revolution —the scientific knowledge explosion with its resulting technological ramifications. But the preoccupation with technology and its instrumentalist view of everybody and everything is raising in our time unavoidable problems about our understanding of man. The very question of man's identity, the conception and conditions of his humanity, and the possibility of avoiding his ultimate destruction all hang upon the devotion of attention and energy to a similar concern for what might be called a humane revolution which will balance and complement the technological one. The present scientific revolution itself is accelerating and threatens to envelope the world in convulsive revolutionary movements in the fields of human rights, race, developing nations, etc. There are not too many signs at present that those in control of society who have benefited most from the technological revolution are aware of the need for massive change in the whole of society, which appears to them to be eminently satisfactory as it is. This may help explain why America, born of revolution,

has increasingly lost sympathy for revolutionary movements and is today unable to cope with their growth
around the world.

Thus it is that we may ask whether we have had too much
change or not enough. Is our age revolutionary enough and
has revolution proceeded in the right directions? Diverse
thinkers.such as Norman O. Brown, Herbert Marcuse, and
Jacques Ellul all raise this question from neo-Freudian,
non-Soviet Marxist, and neo-Protestant points of view.[9]

What is desperately needed is a revolution in the humanities that will permit man to exercise intelligent control
over what his technology now makes possible. Such a
revolution might begin anywhere but it may already have
had its beginnings in the rise of student activism within our
colleges and universities. Such revolution must certainly
find its natural setting within the college because, in addition to the religious communities, it is the college that has
been the nexus for man's attempt to understand not only
his world but himself. The time-honored functions of
liberal education should therefore be reexamined as they
relate to the need and possibility for such a humane
revolution.

2

Twin Goals of a College Education

ADOLESCENCE was, as we have noted, a by-product, or unwitting invention of the industrial revolution. The young age of college students (thirteen to fifteen years) in the seventeenth and eighteenth centuries and the relatively short college course (lasting generally three years) are indications of the rapid maturation expected of young people in nontechnical societies. The age of students also helps explain the background of the traditional parental function of institutions of higher learning. Prior to the nineteenth century there was no real transitional stage between childhood and the assumption of adult responsibilities. The "rites of passage" that briefly marked the transition in primitive societies were represented in the West only by admission to church membership through confirmation. And even this ceremony traditionally took place at the age of nine or ten—only later being moved to the pubertal years of thirteen to fourteen. Indeed, it became impossible that any one rite or ceremony could mark the passage from childhood to maturity in the industrialized societies, because a whole new lengthy stage had intervened. And with the emergence of adolescence a new task was thrust upon the college.

The delay in the assumption of adult roles in society provided time for reflective consideration of fundamental questions regarding man and his place within the cosmos. The recovery of the classical tradition in the Renaissance plus the factor of developing religious pluralism in Western societies meant that no single cultural or philosophical system was regarded as exhausting the storehouse of man's wisdom. The whole of Western society was itself beginning to move in new directions because of the impact of the developing sciences. Thus it was that what is known as an identity crisis became more and more evident in this changed and changing society. New roles for women were also beginning to be explored, and changing patterns of living became characteristic of the expanding middle class. Family relationships shifted as fathers worked at greater distances from the home and, as we have noted, children ceased to be an economic advantage and became financial liabilities.

In these conditions the questions of self-discovery and world discovery became the twin focuses of education. The recent rapid growth of the behavioral sciences, particularly the field of psychology, reflects this burgeoning concern with the understanding of man. But behind the expansion of the traditional curriculum and the exploration of new fields of learning, there lay the implicit, if not always explicit, concern to answer two very ancient questions fundamental to humanity—but now being asked with a new urgency and with new information to go on. The first question is that of man's identity, What is man? or Who am I? The second is the question of what is of supreme worth, or, What is it that I should be willing to give myself up for? Explicit interest in these questions has grown in intensity as young people passing through college have become increasingly aware of the pervasive impact on the understanding of man made by the technological revolution.

It is true that these issues always have been significant questions in the universities of the Western world. They have always been regarded as important, if not the most important, issues to which the educated man could address himself. But, until recent times, they were not the object of much formal debate or concern within particular institutions of higher learning. This was because satisfactory answers to these questions were regarded as already available to the would-be learner. The questions were basic but answers were also at hand. Either the Christian faith or some form of classical humanism provided these answers. But today—with both of these types of commitment on the defensive intellectually—these questions, particularly the first, are being asked with a new sense of urgency. Many of the most promising young people no longer accept the traditional answers that society has provided to these questions as meaningful or relevant to the modern world. One might observe that a strange sort of intellectual application of the law of supply and demand is at work here. The questions have become more precious (at least in the eyes of many students) the scarcer the viable answers are perceived to be.

Since the time immediately following World War II when the vast expansion of college enrollments began, observers of this increasingly important segment of the population have noted that students tended to have a common characteristic. They were said to be naïve existentialists. That is, they were tremendously concerned about the problem of their own identity. They are still asking the question, Who am I? Certainly it must be admitted that no intellectual movement has made as great an impact on the college generation as existentialism has since World War II. This is because students are reacting against that which itself prompted the original existentialist revolt against the philosophical establishment at the end of the nineteenth century, namely, the depersonalization brought about by the encroachment of the technological society on all aspects of human life.

This is not the place to engage in an extensive presentation of existentialism; it is far too complex and diversified a set of movements.[10] But, it is important to note the meaning that lies behind the root of the term "existentialism." In Latin *exstare* means "to stand out." For existentialists this quality of "standing out" is what is unique about man. An object does not stand out, is not exposed or aware. It is all bound up in itself and does not sense its own environment. But man, through his senses, "stands out" to all the world. He is aware just because he lacks the defenses that might protect or isolate him from his environment. Man *must* relate to his world. This is what existentialists mean when they say that for man his existence precedes his essence, that is, man becomes what he is through his capacity to stand out and to choose—to become aware of and responsibly relate to his environment. Thus, in existentialist thought man alone "exists" in a way in which neither God nor objects do.

There are three important senses in which this conception of "standing out" or existence has been meaningful to this generation of college students. The first sense is that of the one who dares separate himself from the crowd. In Greek drama the hero stands out from the chorus. He exists and has an intensity of experience that others do not share. But in the Greek tragedy and the modern novel this existence is often not that of the conquering hero but more frequently that of the tragic figure. There is poignant meaning for young people in a literature that has few traditional heroes. This may be because the elitist conception of the hero has little positive significance to a college generation which, as Dr. Martin Meyerson has stated, is neither the elect nor the electorate. What Dr. Meyerson, the chancellor of New York State University at Buffalo, is pointing to in this phrase is the condition of students today who no longer constitute the elite that students once were. Almost everyone goes to college today. Nor do many students have a vote although they are more aware of political issues than many of those possessing the franchise. Thus, while activist students no longer think of themselves as constituting an intellectual elite, they are aware of themselves as those called upon to stand out and take risks. It is in this sense that they are willing to take leadership in an age of the nonhero.

The second sense in which the existentialist conception of standing out is meaningful to this generation is that of protesting against a depersonalized society and a depersonalizing education. One recalls the oft-repeated story of the college student who commented that the only time his university paid any attention to him was when he bent his IBM card! Students are exceedingly responsive to the negative judgments that those identified with many phases of the existentialist movement have placed upon our technological era. The reactions of protest manifest what appears to be a great deal of cynicism and negativism on the part of activist students. They are not as sure about the kind of society or education that they would want as they are sure that what they are getting does not fill their requirements.

A third conception of *exstare* of significance to many activist students is the way it illuminates the vulnerability that is a characteristic of human life. He who refuses to expose himself, to take the risk of being hurt—in this sense "to stand out"—misses what it is to be human. Existentialist art and literature have dramatically portrayed the exposed and alienated condition of modern man. And significant numbers of students respond to these portrayals and have appropriated this viewpoint—although some have reacted against it. Indeed, as solely a protest movement, existentialism may have already exhausted itself. There are only so many changes that can be rung on the themes of alienation and absurdity. It is not too difficult to predict that although existentialism may have proven an effective tool for social criticism, it lacks what is needed when it comes to constituting a creative intellectual or social force. Nonetheless, the conception of man as vulnerable, surrounded by unfeeling products of the technological society, is firmly established in many of the most sensitive students' minds. To this extent they are and probably will remain indebted to the existentialist movement.

The term "movement," as we noted, should not be applied to existentialism since it is such a diversified set of viewpoints. It is better understood as a stance, an ethos, or a mood. But even as a contributor to the intellectual ethos of our era, the influence of existentialism may be waning largely because of its very vagueness. It does not seem to provide any systematic way of dealing with the problems of our time. This is, of course, one of the problems of any protest movement that does not provide a positive program but rather lives by reaction against the establishment. The so-called "flower power" students who have dropped out still may find in existentialist thought as well as in the more exotic forms of Eastern mysticism resources for their negative way of life. But certainly the activist student groups have found and will probably increasingly find it necessary to go beyond protest existentialism.

Michael Polanyi has noted a particular problem that has been the outgrowth of the relativism which is characterized by some of the major forms of existentialism other than theistic existentialism of say a Tillich or a Maritain. Polanyi observes that the relativizing of all past value systems produces a kind of perfectionism which eventuates either in complete withdrawal from political action or in a form of political action that is perfectionistic and therefore fanatical.[11]

Thus the acceptance of a complete relativist position may be no guarantee against fanaticism. Indeed, it may be all the more dangerous since it recognizes and is frustrated by the subjectivity of its own judgments. Therefore, whatever the dangers of competing ideologies, they do provide an opportunity for discussion between them, as the newly established dialogue between Christian theologians and some Marxist thinkers indicates.[12]

What may be developing on the campuses throughout the Western world is a collision between three kinds of answers to the question of identity. An existentialist answer may be phrased in a modern form of the Cartesian "I think, therefore, I am" expressed "I am, therefore, I suffer." Over against this view is the prevailing concept of technological man which may be expressed in a secularized version of the Protestant work ethic—"I make, therefore, I am." There are interesting implications of this instrumentalist view which will be explored in more detail later. But in addition to other problems, this view would appear to have diminishing applicability in the forthcoming cybernetic era when a few will be able to produce all the goods that society needs. Dr. Murphy, the former chancellor of U.C.L.A. in his final commencement on June 14, 1968, referred to the modern philosophical leitmotiv as expressed in the phrase *Sentio ergo sum,* "I feel, therefore, I am." There are, as Dr. Murphy realizes, problems with this point of view. It may, he notes, turn out to be a kind of anti-intellectualism which values feeling above thinking. But its roots, it may be argued, are not in any self-conscious anti-intellectualism on the part of young people. Rather, it expresses a reaction on their part against a detached type of rationality which, as they point out, seriously games-plays, for example, with the possibility of a nuclear world war. In protest, there is a rising demand among college students for a new type of rationality, one that includes the emotions and involved responsibility for the whole of humanity.

But let us turn to the second question, which is a central issue in all of higher education when it is true to itself. This is the evaluative question as to what it is that is worth the sacrifice of the self. This question may seem, at first consideration, to be antithetical to the question we have just considered, but it has proven, in fact, to be complementary to it. Indeed, in the polarity of these two questions we find an expression of the unique synthesis of Hellenistic and Hebraic elements that have made up that creative cultural amalgam known as Western society. If one strain of the wisdom of Greek society could be summed up by the injunction to "know thyself," then the experience of the Hebraic culture may be said to lie in the recognition that the knowledge of the self is reflexive of the surrender or giving up of self to God and neighbor. "He who would save his life will lose it, and he who will lose his life for my sake will find it." There is in the Bible the strong element of emphasis upon man's creatureliness, his response to the holy which he encounters in the divine. In the dominant Biblical tradition as it is enshrined, for example, in the book of Genesis, man's problem is seen in his desire to answer the question of identity and nature solely on his own terms without reference to God ("You will be *as* gods") and without reference to neighbor ("Am I my brother's keeper?"). Thus the self's preoccupation with itself and its refusal to recognize both its own creatureliness and its relationship to others is, from the Biblical point of view, the root of the human dilemma. In the history of Western philosophical tradition this same question of what draws man outside of himself has been expressed in the spirit of the quest for the good, the true, and the beautiful. It is therefore reflected in the philosophical concern for values. Much modern value theory, however, expresses the ego-centric predicament as dramatically as Genesis' account of the Fall. For many theorists values are defined subjectively and the pervasive relativism of the culture does not permit man to establish what might be "objectively" valuable. Tillich, for example, has attempted to use the term "norm" to express something more than subjective evaluation of persons or the differing evaluations of societies.

Much of modern philosophy has turned away from this thorny issue and has left the field largely in the hands of such social psychologists as Rollo May, Viktor Frankl, and Abraham Maslow. But while the findings of the behavioral sciences must certainly be taken into account by philosophers and theologians, they can hardly reduce themselves solely to restating these findings and still continue to entertain a claim to relevance in the face of the major ethical issues that free men face in the modern world.

In the broader scope we can trace an interesting historical development down the centuries as man has answered the question of what it is for which the individual must sacrifice himself and his personal interests. In primitive societies and in all early human history man apparently felt himself under the dominance of natural forces which he endeavored to understand through unsophisticated personification—the arbitrary power of sea and wind, earthquake and volcano—or, as may be seen in totemism, in the physical and reproductive power of the animal world. This attitude gradually, and in a few select places, gave way to the sense of power of a transcendent Being or beings which expressed themselves through the natural phenomena but were not wholly limited by them or confined to them. This conception provided the foundation for the transcendent value system of the Judeo-Christian religious tradition. While regarding man as a creature, this view set him over against nature because of his alliance with the power that both created and transcended him and the natural world. In the era in which we are now living this transcendence, as has been noted, is being replaced by a new emphasis on immanence. The question remains, however, whether the new humanism that is based upon this immanence will result in a kind of neonaturalism with the worship of the arbitrary power of man, particularly as this is expressed in the technological era, or the subjugation to those elements of man which least yield to rational analysis and control— the will to power and sexuality. There is a disturbing kind of primitivism and almost Dionysian quality to some expressions of the modern spirit.

From the perspective of the Judeo-Christian tradition it is an exceedingly important issue whether this new age of immanence will be able to preserve not the cosmology but some of the unique insights and values of the old transcendent theology. Whether the moral qualities that gradually became attributed to the creator God—the sense of social justice and of personal loving-kindness—can be translated into the immanent value pattern having commanding purchase upon man in this world, remains to be seen. There are signs that among some of the younger generation there may be a struggle to make this the case.

The particular phobia of the young against hypocrisy may be interpreted not as a new discovery of the repulsiveness of this particular human trait, but may be another recognition that—in an era when man must be responsible for his neighbor—hypocrisy stands among the most heinous of human crimes. It is significant to note that while they neither possess nor claim theological sophistication, some of the activists among the student generation certainly reflect in a secular manner the Biblical insight that God identifies himself with those in the community who are most discriminated against by the established powers that be. In the Old Testament a special concern is reflected and legislation promulgated in defense of certain classes of people—the orphans, widows, strangers, and sojourners. God is portrayed as having a special concern for the rights of these groups of people—the ones with the least power within the community. Therefore, from the perspective of the Biblical prophetic tradition, that for which man ought to be willing to sacrifice himself is the rights of those human beings within the present social order who are neglected or forgotten. Society's well-being is bound up with their well-being. (See, for example, Isa., ch. 58.)

There may also be a sense in which many of these student activists are already relating to the problem of self-giving in a more balanced manner than that which has characterized much of the Christian tradition. In some elements of Protestantism the conception of self-surrender has involved a total abhorrence of the self. It was taught that as a depraved sinner one should not love oneself, and the whole motivation for good works was justified by a disregard for self. But many young people today have a better sense of the truth that a person cannot give what he does not have. If he does not value himself or have some sense of dignity, he can hardly bestow these qualities upon others. And man's problem is not that he is an ego but that he becomes an egotist. There is a world of difference between self-regard and egotism. Some young people seem to sense that man cannot love his neighbor properly unless he also has a proper love for himself.

With the consideration of this issue we are brought back to the proper relationship between the two basic questions of self-discovery and self-surrender. It may be asked whether there is a logical or necessary order of priority for these two questions. Is it that I am first to find myself —solve the immediate identity crisis—and then seek some good cause for which I would be willing to sacrifice that which I have found? This procedure has often been considered to be the logical order of things. This view has eventuated in the setting aside of special times and locales for education. Traditionally, there has been a separation from everyday life and an entering upon a special kind of experience, a conception that reflects this priority. As the so-called "rites of passage" of primitive societies frequently take place in settings remote from the normal life of the tribe—so the identity question of the young within Western culture has been given a special location, the college with its campus. One might even go farther with this analogy. Just as in primitive tribes priests and shamans preside over these puberty rites, so educators are asked to preside over the equally mystifying tests which make a young man or a young woman a mature member of Western society. Dr. Hans Hoffman has commented that there has been almost a mystical conception of what transpires within teacher-training institutions, theological seminaries, etc. He notes that society has felt the need and so has provided for the production of teachers, ministers, etc. But society has been equally mystified about how one acquires the ability to teach or to minister. Thus it has provided means whereby people are sent away to special locations and put through a series of courses and training after which it was possible to ascribe to them the particular powers society required.

There are a number of theoretical objections, of course, to be raised as to the order of priority we are exploring. There are many possible answers to the questions of identity which could be dealt with almost interminably. And it has been observed that our educational system does create students who possess many opinions but few convictions. For one thing, without some actual practical situation in which to try out a world view or a conception of the self, it is impossible to know what the most satisfactory view might be.

The contemporary student generation is also engaged in a rather violent protest against the view of the college as a place of detachment, objectivity—the ivory tower image of education. Certainly the commitments of the student generation may not have the traditional characteristics of endurance and totality which one associates with much of the Western cultural heritage. Students, however, are still making commitments although of a different kind. They are more flexible, their intensities change, but they are commitments nonetheless. What is more, they spring not only from the academic study of value traditions but also from exposure to the social dilemmas of a society that has an official allegiance to democratic freedoms but whose actual life is far from fully consistent with the commitments that it declares.[13]

One might say that many of the most active students appear to want to reverse the order in which the two fundamental questions have traditionally been asked and answered. They seem—in a cavalier disregard for their careers, reputations, parental goodwill, etc.—to be prepared to throw away their lives for a cause. Many of them seem to be overly anxious to take the risk, thinking that this kind of sacrifice will answer their own identity question even if it will not solve the problems they are addressing themselves to. Actually, there is some evidence to support this viewpoint in the practical experience of society. The person who is thrown into a situation for which he is totally unprepared but which demands much of him frequently finds himself responding creatively to such a challenge. The notion of risk, so precious within the official value pattern of our society but so seldom followed, has great appeal to the idealism of youth.

But one of the problems with the "school of hard knocks" kind of approach is that one may sacrifice oneself to a cause without seeing that cause in relationship to the claims of the total environment. One might well find oneself devoted to something less worthy than other kinds of commitments that one might have made. Just jumping on one of the many bandwagons that throng our campuses does not permit the careful analysis of options in which a person involved in higher education ought to be engaged. It must be admitted, however, that those who have found themselves thrust into such circumstances have sometimes found the motivation to return to their studies with a renewed zeal. But the risks are high.

Obviously the most desirable answer to the question of priority in relationship to the questions of identity and self-surrender lies in a simultaneity—or as nearly simultaneous as possible in dealing with both problems. It is imperative that this kind of education transform the curricula of colleges and universities. Programs that permit students to study the various conceptions of man and values within the world and to relate these to the experience of some of the great issues of our time (race, poverty, population explosion, etc.) must become commonplace rather than the exception. Such a transformation would mean that colleges and universities must expand their limited contacts within their communities and engage in more cooperative efforts than the present limited consortia provide.

One danger to avoid at all costs is by-passing or ignoring two fundamental questions because they are so difficult to deal with or because they seem to claim time and effort from tasks more immediately practical and possible. Archibald MacLeish has written: "What is happening, and in the greatest universities as well as in the less great, is that the entire educational process is becoming fixed—hung-up as the phrase goes now—on its vocational end result. The job out there in the profession or the industry dictates the 'training' (their word, not mine) in the graduate schools, and the graduate schools dictate the preparation in the colleges, and the whole system congeals from the top down like a pond freezing. The danger is that society may congeal with it, for nothing is more certain in the history of our kind than the fact that frozen societies perish.

"As specialized, professional training, higher education in the United States today is often magnificent. Young doctors are better and better as their specialties become more specialized: so much better that it is now a recommendation in almost any field to say of a young doctor that he is young. Student physicists in the great graduate schools are so notoriously productive at twenty-two that a professional physicist of thirty regards himself, or is regarded by his juniors, as middle-aged. But the educated *man*, the man capable not of providing specialized answers, but of asking the great and liberating questions by which humanity makes its way through time, is not more frequently encountered than he was two-hundred years ago. On the contrary, he is rarely discovered in public life at all."[14]

Just because maintaining the ever more complex machines of the technological, cybernated era demands so much time and talent, there is the real possibility that the adult world which supports higher education may turn away from the traditional concerns of the liberal arts college. Certainly the temper of the student generation would indicate that young people will not settle for continuing the present state of affairs. A student concern for such immediately impractical human endeavors as folk music, art of all kinds, and philosophical and religious meditation may provide the impetus to restore something of a needed balance in our society. The model for our social structures will increasingly appear more organic than mechanical. Then, also, in a curious way even our scientific studies are bringing us back to an organic rather than instrumentalist understanding of man and his problems. The ecological crisis that we are about to examine demonstrates this clearly.

3

Education and the Ecological Crisis: Religious Roots and Ramifications

IT WAS PROBABLY to be expected that the rapidly industrializing Western European society in the eighteenth and nineteenth centuries should produce a view of the universe modeled after its greatest invention, the machine. Philosophers from Descartes to Leibniz and scientists under the dominance of Newton looked upon the harmony they discovered in nature and saw it operating after the pattern of a great, smoothly working machine.

From what is regarded as the beginning of modern philosophy, Descartes separated reality into two kinds: *res extensa* (extended things), which could be measured and with which the developing sciences dealt, and *res cogitans* (thinking substance), not measurable, a kind of mirror reflecting man's vision of the world. This latter field was the proper concern of philosophy and religion. The result of this division was that attention came to be concentrated almost wholly in that sphere where exact calculation, manipulation, and control so quickly brought tangible results. Reinhold Niebuhr has noted that one of the reasons for the triumph of science was the precision and the usefulness of the symbols with which it dealt. The religious images were more vague and far from leading to possible control, competition between them had involved man in a disastrous series of wars.[15] Thus, in Western society there gradually grew up the idea that if it isn't matter, it doesn't matter. The truth is that matter seemed to operate like a machine. This idea is one of the roots of a development which increasingly separated matter from spirit, fact from value, religion from science. It is instructive to note that this machine model was characteristic of the earliest modern science, particularly the field of physics, and gradually spread from there to other fields. But scientists have been gradually forced to abandon this machine model, first in the field of physics and now in other fields of science as well. There is, however, great reluctance on the part of many to admit the problems which the machine model poses in coming to an understanding of man today. Indeed, some of the most exciting and disturbing scientific developments going on find scientists attacking this machine model, a product of the technological era, as no longer adequate for their own disciplines. Werner Heisenberg has stated, "The old division of the world into objective processes in space and time and the mind in which these processes are mirrored—in other words, the Cartesian difference between *res cogitans* and *res extensa*—is no longer a suitable starting point for our understanding of modern science."[16]

The scientific machine model, perhaps the most elusive but pervasive of all the products of the technological era, is even more disastrous when applied to psychology, social science, and political science than it has been when applied to modern physics. The machine model approach tends to treat men as if they were machines. And it is against this very attitude that many of our most sensitive college students are protesting. Indeed, the inefficiency and lack of logic which sometimes characterizes youth's protest are indications of their rejection of efficiency as an ultimate value and the present order as the best obtainable.

The machine model involves a conception of man's relationship to the physical world in which the mind discovers so-called laws which govern the operation of the universe and then applies these laws in such a way as to control the universe. Wresting the secret of nature from nature, that is, discovering the mechanism of its operations, man is able to tame nature and make it subservient to his will. This approach obviously involves increasing the gap which already has long existed between man and nature and which can be traced back to elements in Greek philosophy as well as to the influence of the Biblical conception of man as a special creation set within the natural world. In this viewpoint, man is not a part of nature but is separated from nature, and it is man's divinely bestowed rationality that is seen as the means by which man can triumph over his natural environment.

In the theology of the nineteenth-century German Albrecht Ritschl this viewpoint received its classic formulation. Although this theology was that against which almost all modern theologians such as Barth and Tillich have reacted, Ritschl is still important for a number of reasons. He attempted to synthesize faith and reason, religion and culture, by carving out in the field of morals a realm for religion that could not be taken away by advancement within the field of the sciences and yet which would add to and complement man's scientific pursuits. According to Ritschl, following Kant, man's mind was competent in its own restricted field, that is, in dealing with knowledge of the world. Religion, however, still had its place providing the value systems and the morals by which rational men could order their lives within the world. Thus rationality and morality worked together to subdue the natural order bringing it under the control of enlightened men. Religion should continue to be valued as the means by which man increases his control over his own nature and is able to determine his moral conduct in the world. For Ritschl, Christianity was the highest religion because of the superlative nature of its moral code and the way in which it had contributed to the rise of the dominant bourgeois civilization.

A popularized form of Ritschl's theology informed much of Protestantism and was communicated to middle-class America in the early part of the twentieth century. Ritschl's ideas provided the background for the common conception that religion is a matter of practical morality and that while differences in doctrines may persist, one can be indifferent to them since doctrine is peripheral. Thus denominational differences are viewed as a matter of historical accident and Christianity is regarded as another support for the American way of life. This liberal religion also helped give rise to what is proving to be a fallacious view of man in relationship to his physical environment. If one accepted this point of view, in the world of nature man was seen to exhibit a magnificent competence, even if in his own world of human society man was admittedly incompetent. The explanation of this paradox was said to be that man was competent in the realm of science because no value judgments were demanded there, but he was incompetent in dealing with other human beings because this did require the adjustment between personal values and social good. More attention, the argument goes, should be given to religion so that it might "catch up" to science.

This model of man as the conqueror of nature yet the victim of his own moral incompetence no longer would seem to be a viable one. What is being termed the "ecological crisis" is giving the lie to this conception. Indeed, the contrast between man's technological competence over nature and his ethical ineptitude with regard to his own species is only an apparent difference. Articles appearing in the professional journals, television, newspapers, and magazines, as well as on radio, make it increasingly obvious that men are blind not only with respect to their relationship with other human beings but also to important aspects of the natural world as well. Human survival is threatened not only by a growing social crisis but also by a technological crisis. It is important to understand the interrelationship between these crises if we are to understand something of what lies behind some aspects of student protest and if we are to stave off disaster. The renewal of college education involves a careful consideration of this ecological crisis so that man may utilize the new powers of science and technology he already possesses to improve the human condition. Pollution of our environment is just beginning to capture the attention it deserves.[17]

Barry Commoner, the chairman of the department of botany and director of the Center for the Biology of Natural Systems of Washington University, has stated, "The rapid deterioration of the environment in which we live has become a chief determinant of the quality of our lives. We all know the dismal list: air pollution, pollution of water by urban and industrial wastes and by runoff of farmland fertilizer, multiple hazards of widespread dissemination of insecticides, herbicides, and fungicides, radiation hazards from fallout due to nuclear testing, and—for the future, if we make the catastrophic blunder—the consequences for the biology of man, beast, and plant of massive nuclear, chemical, and biological weapons of modern war."[18] Dr. Commoner noted in his address that we used to be told that nuclear testing was perfectly harmless. Only now, after the damage has been done, we know differently. Commoner cited the contrast between statements of two American Presidents with respect to nuclear testing. In 1956 President Eisenhower said, "The continuance of the present rate of H-bomb testing, by the most sober and responsible scientific judgment, does not imperil the health of man." But as Commoner has noted, in 1964 President Johnson said of the new test-ban treaty: "This treaty has halted the steady, menacing increase of radioactive fallout. The deadly products of atomic explosions were poisoning our soil, our food and the milk our children drank, and the air we all breathe. Radioactive deposits were being formed in increasing quantity in the teeth and bones of young Americans. Radioactive poisons were beginning to threaten the safety of people throughout the world. They were a growing menace to the health of every unborn child." The fact is that, at the insistence of the military, scientists exploded bombs before they really knew the consequences. But it is also true that our technological society produced power plants and automobiles that have enveloped cities in smog before anyone knew the harmful effects of such pollution. Chemists synthesized new insecticides before they learned that they would also kill birds and might be harmful to people. Chemists produced detergents and industry invested millions of dollars in sales promotion putting billions of pounds into the surface waters of our country before it was realized that sewage systems could not break down these compounds and that they would pollute our streams. One could go on listing a record of serious failures in man's recent encounter with his natural environment. After a survey of this, one would come to the logical conclusion that man is really no more competent to deal with nature than he is with himself. Thus the myth of man ascendant over nature is exploded.

One of the great needs of our time is the reassessment of our attitude toward the natural world. This attitude is largely and indeed originally was the product of religious commitment.[19] So again we face the issue that it is the educated and scientifically developed nations which threaten the world, not the so-called primitive people. This is because an almost fatal illusion has been fostered in technological societies and this illusion is that modern man has escaped from his dependence upon the balance of nature. The truth, however, is precisely the opposite. Man has become not less dependent on the balance of nature but more so. And modern technology has left little leeway in the ecological system. Unless men begin to match their technological power with the deeper understanding of the balance of nature, they run the risk of destroying the planet as a suitable place for human habitation. Increasing numbers of young people sense this fact and are dubious about the reckless abandon of putting more and more products on the market in order to foster our affluent American way of life. With the burgeoning world population explosion and a deteriorating physical environment, they are sensitive to the problematic world that technology is bequeathing to their generation.

As we have said, there are definite religious roots to this ecological problem. This is because there is a connection between the rise of science and technology in the Western world and the Judeo-Christian religious heritage. As part of the total ethos of Western culture, certain basic claims about God, man, and the world were affirmed which were also conducive to the development of the scientific methodology and outlook.[20] First, there was the belief that God was immanent within and yet transcendent over the world. This meant that man might experiment with nature without running the risk of impiety. Secondly, there was the affirmation that the world was created *ex nihilo* so that it could have been other than it is. Thus the world could not be completely known by the processes of deduction as much Greek philosophy had claimed, but inductively by observing it and experimenting with it. Also the book of Genesis saw man's special role as that of having dominion over the creative order. Man was to tend the Garden of Eden, and the intellectual work of classification may even be hinted at in the episode of God accepting man's names for the animals. Technologists operating within primitive cultures have been amazed to find that the root of some of their labor problems is fundamentally religious. Natives sometimes objected to the use of dynamite and bulldozers in dealing with nature because of their understanding of the intimate relationship between spiritual powers and the physical universe. In some of these instances Western technicians for the first time became aware of the fact that their Judeo-Christian heritage played a decisive role with respect to the common Western understanding of man's physical environment. Christian apologists, such as John Baillie and Charles Hartshorne, have been at pains to point out this relationship between Christian faith and Western science and have congratulated our religious tradition for its magnificent contribution to our physical comfort and rising standard of living. But this is something like congratulating us for the Protestant work ethic in an era threatened by the mass unemployment that may be brought about by cybernation. The ecological crisis is certainly not that of which we ought to be unduly proud. The church must seriously reexamine its contribution to the ecological dilemma that we face.

The interest that many young people have in the Eastern religions may be a recognition on their part that these faiths have not been partners in deteriorating the natural environment. As the pervasive modern influence of Japanese architecture indicates, oriental cultures have an ancient tradition of a sensitive cooperation between man and his physical environment. But by separating man from the world and making the world a mere thing to be used by men for their own ends, Western religions have helped precipitate a crisis of alienation. Particularly Protestantism, by centering its almost exclusive attention on the subjective relationship between God and man in the innermost recesses of the soul, has contributed to the devaluation of the material world. The contemporary theological preoccupation with a Buberian I-Thou relationship has produced a distorted view of the physical world. Martin Buber's Judaism with its rich use of symbolic objects and physical actions provided a better balance for this almost exclusive emphasis upon the personal. But, in the hands of Protestants whose conception of the sacramental is somewhat deficient, the result has been to increase man's sense of alienation from his physical environment. More than three decades ago Paul Tillich pointed out that the manipulation of things by technical man without adequate attention being paid to their true structure has brought about an ironic revenge in the turning of men into things. Unintentionally, the machine-based economy has increased the feeling of being depersonalized so that individuals sense themselves to be cogs in a machine or punched IBM cards.[21] In a most stimulating article published in a number of journals, Dr. Lynn White, Jr., of the history department at U.C.L.A., has noted both how late in human history and how unique has been the marriage of science and technology.[22] It is this synthesis, he notes, that has resulted in the Baconian affirmation that knowledge is power. That this conjunction occurred under the aegis of Western and not Eastern Christianity, White observes, only indicates how complex Christian faith is and how it reacts differently in different cultural contexts. He states: "The Greeks believed that sin was intellectual blindness, and that salvation was found in illumination, orthodoxy—that is, clear thinking. The Latins, on the other hand, felt that sin was moral evil, and that salvation was to be found in right conduct. Eastern theology has been intellectualist. Western theology has been voluntarist. The Greek saint contemplates; the Western saint acts. The implications of Christianity for the conquest of nature would emerge more easily in the Western atmosphere."[23]

It might prove intriguing to speculate upon the implications of this Western Christian outlook on the development of institutions of higher learning in Europe. We have already alluded to George Williams' identification of a pervasive theme in Biblically influenced cultures which might be termed the "restored Garden of Eden motif."[24] It is this theme that provided the motivation for founding many institutions of higher learning. Particularly, as Williams documents it, was this theme important in the prolific creation of American colleges whose initiators felt they were bringing order into the midst of chaos as they cultivated seminaries of learning in the Western wilderness. Other writers have elaborated on the garden theme which is visually symbolized in the tradition of the college quadrangle with its green campus. But we have been insisting that the conditions of the modern world—so largely the creation of the technological revolution—have made this closed, isolated, and sequestered setting for higher education no longer viable or desirable. The infiltration of the world into the city seen in the envelopment of campus after campus by the urban sprawl, has spelled the end to the isolated garden theme. Polluted air, urban noise, and frustrated inhabitants of the ghettos all leap over the once-protective walls of colleges and universities. And what many American institutions of higher learning are now discovering—that there is no place to hide—the suburbs will soon discover. Now either the whole society is the focus for redemption or none of it. But perhaps the verdant campuses, bequeathed by tradition, may be given new meaning if they can symbolize the ecological responsibility of colleges and universities for the whole of the society in which they live and function.

If the ancient idea so important in the genesis of colleges, that the chaos of human alienation and sin may be overcome, at least in part, by the disciplines of study, is to have any continuing significance, it must be expanded in such a way that the narrowly conceived ecological responsibility symbolized by the campus extends to assisting in the creation of a renewed and human urban environment.

Lynn White has maintained that within Western Christianity the only tradition that stands against the religiously rooted deprecation of inanimate nature is that represented by Francis of Assisi. And the idea which underlay Francis' conception of kinship with nature was his regard for humility, not just as a private virtue, but one desirable for all mankind. In the Biblical heritage man's primal sin is seen as pride. Made possible by man's superlative endowments, it is this pride that in the Genesis myth of Creation tempted man to exaggerate his position in relation to the Creator and to his fellowman. But the same story hints at an early expression of the ecologic problem in its reference to the disastrous effects in the natural world that were occasioned by human sin. (See Gen. 3:18; 4:12.)

In the thought of Francis, nature was not, as Dr. White notes, simply a series of homilies, an illustrated book of pious notions, nor, we might observe, was it simply the sounding board for contact between man and God which it became in later Thomist thought. Rather, it was a brother creation with man which praises God in its ways as man does in his. Those who are familiar with Francis' "Canticle of the Sun" know how close was the identification he felt with inanimate nature.

The church dealt harshly with the "panpsychism" of Francis as may be seen in its rejection of the conception of the animal soul. But today some theologians are attempting to do something to redress this wrong. Although his focus is almost exclusively upon the development of man as the highest expression of the evolutionary process, the works of the great French Jesuit paleontologist Teilhard de Chardin have Franciscan overtones. In his writings man's genesis is set firmly within the great processes of nature of which he is a part and for which man is increasingly responsible. The widespread interest in Teilhard is an indication itself of the hunger for a meaningful understanding of the physical universe, a dominant characteristic of our time. It is interesting to note that a very high percentage of those in the rather large number of Teilhard de Chardin study groups are scientists and technicians. It would appear that they are most sensitive to the metaphysical roots of the ecologic problem and are searching for some means of redressing a balance which they sense has been upset by the way in which their own professions operate. Thus we can hope that there will be an increase in the sensed need to improve upon the common cultural understanding of nature.

As a young person matures in our society the whole matter of developing an appreciation and responsibility for man's physical environment should be an important part of his developing aesthetic awareness. The field of aesthetics, indeed, must be given increased attention in formal education. And since aesthetics is important to city and regional planning, an ecological sensitivity should be cultivated and related to the science of politics. This means that the twin questions of identity and self-giving on the college level must be treated in the light of such radically new problems as the cybernetic revolution with its threat to the conception of man solely as one who works and the ecological crisis which has been the fruit of a view of man solely as the exploiter of nature.

White argues that the present technological era is shot through with human arrogance toward nature and that this arrogance has its origins in Christianity. He is pessimistic, therefore, as to whether there are resources in any of the contemporary widespread expressions of Christian faith to meet the challenge represented by the ecological crisis. Perhaps, we may say, this is what many young people sense, particularly those who are turning to various forms of Eastern religious thought. White is clear, however, in that since the origin of the crisis is largely religious, whether formally recognized as such or not, the solutions must also be religious, whether they will be recognized as such or not. Thus he closes his observations with the injunction that "we must rethink and refeel our nature and destiny."

One of the characteristics of the crisis of our era is its scope. No one problem, such as the ecological one, can be dealt with in isolation, but it necessarily involves all others. We have seen that the problem of the identity of the self cannot be separated from the problem of the nature of human community. And the problems of man as an individual and in community cannot be treated apart from the problem of the total environment and the impact upon it of his technology. Both of these issues, then, relate directly to the rising tide of demand for the fruits of technology among the disadvantaged at home and abroad. The future of human life on this planet demands the simultaneous solution to all these problems and many more. The massiveness, therefore, of the difficulties faced and the complexity of the factors we have noted, necessitate a radical change in American education. Particularly must liberal arts colleges be aware of these issues and reflect them in every aspect of life from curriculum reform to dormitory-planning. Whether the colleges have the resources to respond to the apparently overwhelming problems is a question that must be faced. Perhaps the despair and indifference displayed by many young people are reflections of an ethos that they sense among faculty and others in the colleges.

But the whole matter of a radical reassessment of thought and feeling, which White calls for, returns us to the problem that we have alluded to a number of times and which must be faced in any reappraisal of the proper functioning of institutions of higher learning. This is the situation expressed by the seeming rejection on the part of the student generation of a type of intellectualism and an apparent flight into immediate sense experience. The "now" generation is explicitly and implicitly directing a major criticism upon the important place traditionally given to detached objective reasoning. It is this objectivity that separates thought from feeling and actions from their effects which, they appear to be saying, has produced a depersonalized technological society that is more concerned for gadgets than men and is indifferent to the growing ecological crisis.

4

The Sensate Generation: Intellectual Objectivity vs. Immediate Experience

IN THE LONG HISTORY of the race the formalization of education may be seen as a process that has involved the rejection of the dominance of immediate experience. It is a function that has increasingly been devoted to the refinement or sifting of sense impressions, leading to an increased control by man of his environment. This has been accomplished through the twin disciplines of detachment and reflection. From the early Greek philosophers the world as it appears has been identified with illusion, and reality was said to be known only by a laborious process involving the reordering of what was given immediately in sense experience. This, of course, is the origin of the time-honored distinction between appearance and reality. Thus education (*e-ducere*, to lead out) has been thought of as that which leads man out of the world of illusions.

Many young people today, however, are undertaking a revolt against the detachment that they have identified with objectivity. They are reasserting the need for direct experience. This is because many of them regard this mood of detachment, which they increasingly have identified with the educated man, as one of the signs of sickness in our society. Most students are not very clear as to why they are reacting so violently against detachment or academic objectivity. For some of them this revolt is generated by a resentment against the increasing length of time spent in preparation for adult life. Once in our society, high school was regarded as sufficient preparation; now college is a requirement for almost all. Soon graduate work will be as common as college once was. This means that the time in which real life begins seems to be constantly receding before the demands for more training. The postponement of the taking up of adult roles increases young people's sense of detachment from life.

Some students see the stress on detachment and objectivity as the heart of man's alienation from the physical world—that which has produced the ecological crisis as well as increasing man's sense of alienation from his fellowman with the resultant political crisis. Man, these students say, has thought so much that he has lost the capacity to feel. Thus, they complain, we have produced a so-called "rational" society whose goals are manifestly insane and which is typified by the mad scientist Dr. Strangelove. Many young people find meaningful Mahatma Gandhi's comment that what troubled him most about post-independence India was the hardheartedness of her intellectuals.

The widespread experimentation with drugs on the part of high school and college young people is an unavoidable indication of this frantic search for direct experience. Hallucinogens are looked upon as valuable because they produce a unique and vivid experience. If this experience is similar to the classical religious experience, then it has an exotic attraction as a protest against a so-called rational society and is guaranteed to scandalize the adult generation. Marshall McLuhan has expressed the need for what he calls a "haptic balance," that is, the harmonious comprehension of the world by all the senses man possesses. McLuhan claims that this haptic balance was seriously upset by the invention of printing, so that our culture is now excessively visual. Moreover, printing, utilizing as it does uniform and repeatable symbols, has contributed to the reduction of the world to the machine model. We might therefore speculate that some young people are using drugs in order to restore this haptic balance. Indeed, one theory of how LSD works is that it incapacitates the selection mechanism of the middle brain which determines which stimuli one is going to pay attention to. With this selector out of action all sense experiences appear to be as strong as that upon which one normally concentrates— hence, the vividness of the "trip" experience.

In his important study of general education Daniel Bell has pointed to the increased desire for direct experience on the part of young people, and he stresses their impatience with many of the traditional disciplines of higher education. Bell expresses a vague hope that young people may come to understand the wisdom of the mature—that discipline increases both the freedom and the ability to experience. It must be admitted that the reason behind the hard work involved in mastering certain methodologies has not been made very clear to young people by most educators. Every opportunity must be used to make evident that the experience which young people seek is all the more vivid and meaningful when it has been reflected upon and refined by the use of certain disciplines. But the situation is something like the church's traditional prohibition against premarital sex. For many young people this attitude has seemed to stem from organized Christianity's fear of sex and the experiences which express it. Few Christian moralists have been able to relate their teachings about sexual responsibility to a rationale of that which makes sex itself more meaningful, valuable, and pleasurable.

In the light of growing student protest against the postponement of pleasures and the widespread search for new kinds of direct experience, it is important that educators reexamine some of the factors that have led to a separation of education from direct experience in life. This reexamination may lead in the direction of increasing interrelatedness between experience and reflection upon it. A brief exploration of the history of the concept of detachment as basic to education brings us face to face with those factors which have contributed to the genesis and rise of the natural sciences. And this development is a very specific historical process repeated nowhere else, although its results are now being spread everywhere through the westernization of world culture.

The scientific method was another product of that decisive blending of Hebraic and Hellenistic elements which produced a culture which in its technological orientation every society in the world is imitating.[25]

It has been noted that one distinctive difference between the Hebraic and Hellenistic cultures lies in the approach to knowledge characteristic of each. For the Hebrew to know is to become involved with, committed to—as the use of the verb *yådå* (to know), which might appear to be merely a euphemism for sexual relations, indicates. The Greeks were the initiators of the detached approach to knowledge, for the Hellenistic philosophical tradition taught that one knew something by standing back and observing it. The intellect was the tool by which man could distinguish appearance from reality. It was man's mind that separated him from the rest of nature and enabled him to objectify the world. It is deceptively simple to conclude that if this means that the Hebraic approach to knowledge is subject-oriented and the Greek object-oriented, the solution is to have both. But this does not really take into account the dominant influence upon modern man and his almost exclusive preoccupation with objective knowledge brought about by the success of the sciences in increasing his capacity to deal with his environment.

Paul Tillich has noted that one of the presuppositions of science is that through its methods man confronts the world but retains an "attitude of distance"—a detachment from it.[26] James Luther Adams, in commenting on Tillich's point, states that "negatively [it implies] that there is some element of deception involved in the attitude of pure immediacy, and it implies positively that something dependable can be arrived at by the scientific attitude of distance. This positive implication is, however, a matter of faith; it is the faith that precedes all science and that is itself not grounded scientifically, even though it may find confirmation in innumerable instances.[27] Thus at the genesis of scientific knowledge there lies the very ancient supposition that things are not what they appear to be in the immediacy of their experience—a white cow under a tree is not really gray although it appears to be, and a straight stick immersed in a glass beaker is not bent though it looks it. Here also is the root of the faith that detachment from immediate experience, bringing to bear sources of reflection and memory, can overcome the naïve deceptions of the senses. This idea expressed in varying degrees of sophistication is not only Greek in origin but a common discovery in all cultures insofar as men reflect upon their environment. But only in the West did this idea, under the impact of the Judeo-Christian faith, result in the explosive growth of scientific knowledge.

This idea derived from early Greek philosophy has been the constant presupposition of Western education. Reality was viewed as lying beneath the surface of things and to be sought through some form of rigor or discipline. This was as much a presupposition of the artist as of the natural scientist. But, it is noted, the artist has not only used techniques of objectivity but generally has also striven to penetrate into the mystery of his object by involving himself with it or by approaching it by the means of intuition. The scientist, however, was thought to use only the method of distancing himself from the object of his attention. It may, however, be asked whether this distinction is really valid. For while it may characterize the attitude of some scientists (what one could pejoratively refer to as technoscientists), it certainly does not describe the attitude of many of the most creative scientists of past and present. Many scientists take a position that is much closer to that ascribed to the artist. While not refusing to acknowledge the importance of the immediate experience of things, they have sought to penetrate to their core—to their essences—in, beyond, with, and behind the immediate experience. This is the fascinating history of Western man's changing conception of the structure of meaning (the logos) which is, as Tillich taught, found uniquely in every object of knowledge.

Paul Tillich devoted much of his writings to the exploration of this particular development. He has shown the process by which the logos—the meaning structure—which was originally sought by the mystical philosopher for the sake of contemplating its beauty—came to be valued because it provided the means by which man's environment could be controlled. In Stoicism the first major philosophical movement of the ancient Western world to exert widespread influence in the culture, the ascetic disciplines were to be cultivated, since through them there was opened up a universe of harmonious design with which one could become united in mystic contemplation. The logos was thus conceived to be the means by which man might come to know the goodness, truth, and beauty of the cosmos. In the history of Western culture, Francis Bacon's conception that "knowledge is power" at first gradually, then swiftly, replaced the conception of logos as beauty to be contemplated with the idea that it was power to be used. The rational structures became the means by which man might manipulate and control the universe. This is the origin of the development in which only so much reality was granted to things as their usefulness demanded. This process entailed the reduction of the conception of the logos to a distinctly utilitarian dimension expressed in the commercial value of things. For Tillich this change in the way in which the logos was conceived has been the source of so many of the ills of contemporary society. Herein, for example, lie the roots of the alienation of the artist from society. This is also the real problem Tillich sees with even the modified, humane, modern capitalism, that is, the way in which it stifles the resources of sensitivity and creativity among those whom it benefits by depriving them of whole dimensions of reality. Herein also lies the basis of the ecological crisis—the refusal of man to respect the logos structures expressed uniquely in all the objects of his environment. This conception of the logos may also be the source of the malaise that infects our educational system where learning is valued not only for its own sake or what it enables a person to be but primarily for what it enables us to do. Tillich refers to the process of the loss of the depth dimension in our culture. He does not, of course, advocate a return to a mere mystical contemplative society based on the ancient's view of the logos. But he is concerned about the failure of our present society to include what the mystics understood about man's relationship to his world. There is loss involved both when the logos is a source of contemplation alone, as in Eastern mysticism, or for control alone as in modern technological society. The logos structures could be appreciated for both in what Tillich refers to as a theonomous society.

The educational process of detachment and discipline for the sake of discovering the meaning (logos) could also include valuing things because of their uniqueness. There is no necessary opposition between sensitive appreciation and appropriate use, as the artists constantly remind us. Tillich refers to the manner in which both man and the material world are fulfilled in the process of the creative act. In this act man respects the logos as expressed within the materials he uses. His work makes those structures more evident and both the object and man find meaning in this act. Thus the artisan who selects a piece of wood for its fine grain and polishes it in such a way that the pattern is made more beautiful and who uses it for some purpose clearly fulfills the logos in the wood and in himself. This type of act should characterize the relationship that man has with his whole physical environment producing a true ecology of mutual fulfillment and meaning.

We have mentioned before the importance to some of the more politically involved student activists of the writings of Herbert Marcuse. A professor at the University of California in San Diego, Marcuse is a non-Soviet Marxist philosopher. His background is startlingly similar to Tillich's, and he comes to many of the same conclusions in his analysis of technological society. Neither writer, interestingly enough, pays much attention to the other. The subject of one of Marcuse' better-known works, *One-Dimensional Man,* focuses upon a society that has lost its critical dimension—an idea found constantly in Tillich's writing.[28] Developing their thought independently, both Tillich and Marcuse concur in faulting the one-plane limitations of the technological reason. They agree that this shallowness has brought about the major illnesses of contemporary society. Marcuse appears to have more direct influence upon the political expression of the student activist groups than Tillich. This may be because he is a more recent "discovery" than Tillich whose works have been used for years in a wide variety of college courses. Perhaps Marcuse' avowed Marxism has more shock value than the muted Marxism of Tillich's "out-of-date" religious socialism. Marcuse, whose works are banned in the Soviet Union, has expressed a "plague on both your houses" position also found in many alienated youth with respect to East-West relations, while Tillich grew more tolerant of the establishment before he died.

Marcuse sees in the development of empiricist philosophy the furthering of a fallacious view of man's knowledge of his world. There is a strong element of British empiricism present in the modern practical instrumentalist viewpoint, which Marcuse claims is under the control of an oligarchic establishment. He contends that for empiricism the function of man's reason was to provide accurate knowledge of the exterior world as it really was. Reason was viewed as giving man facts; but reflecting strong nominalist roots, empiricism denied reality to any universal or general ideas. These, Marcuse notes, were claimed to be the products of man's invention. In the knowledge situation all that we were really bound to was the givenness of the data so that the function of reason became purely technical.

As a Marxist, Marcuse is committed to changing the present order of things. Knowledge of the real world is not merely for the sake of adjustment to facts as they are but is a means for changing the world. This change is not merely subjective or arbitrary, however, but should be devoted toward remaking the world after the demands of Reason, which Marcuse spells with a capital R. Marcuse therefore finds in the empiricist-pragmatist tradition something that must be modified by the appreciation of a reevaluated idealism.[29] Marcuse also finds in the plea for realism in the "commonsense" school the modern expression of the empiricist tradition. And he excoriates linguistic analysis because its approach accepts reality as a brute fact and denigrates philosophy into a slavish servant of technological science. He is furious at "Wittgenstein's assurance that philosophy 'leaves everything as it is'."[30] He writes, "Such statements exhibit, to my mind, academic sado-masochism, self-humiliation, and self-denunciation of the intellectual whose labor does not issue in scientific, technical or like achievements."[31]

The end result of the empiricist-pragmatist-positivist development has been the creation of societies as we know them—which Marcuse describes as being instrumentalist or operationalist. In these societies, capitalist and communist, a person or a thing is defined solely by what he or it does. Marcuse argues that every aspect of our society has been infected by this outlook, including the very language by which we seek to communicate.

The *status quo*—maintained by great effort on the part of the establishment—inevitably reflects this machine model of reality. Marcuse also notes that it was physics that first gave rise to the instrumentalist position but which now is making us aware of the severe limitations of the machine model when applied to science today. Now that it is no longer possible for physicists to conceive reality ac-

cording to pictorial models, it has also become impossible
to maintain that human knowledge provides us with an
objective model of reality as it really is. Despite the fact
that Immanuel Kant demonstrated this two centuries ago,
only now is it being recognized by many scientists that
we alter what we observe by observing it and that we can
never know the world as it is in itself. As Marcuse notes,
the knowledge relationship is a "project," that is, that
learning affects the world that is learned and that the projection itself reflects the commitments and purposes of the
one knowing.

What all of this means to the activist student leadership
who have read Marcuse and appropriated many of his
ideas is that all of our scientific knowledge and the present
educational system itself is shaped by a clandestine commitment to things as they are. Only a radical new understanding of how man knows and a radical transformation
of his institutions of knowledge, they then argue, will be
able to free men from the pervasive instrumentalist ethos
which the machine model has fostered and maintains.

Marcuse' answer to the dilemma of the one-dimensional
society that he finds in both East and West involves revolutionary change. So massive is the transition proposed that
from the perspective of the establishment (American and
Soviet) the program appears to threaten nothing less than
chaos and nihilism. But alarming as it is, Marcuse' solution
is certainly less drastic than that advocated by another
one of the heroes of the student activists, Norman O.
Brown. Brown seeks a complete overturning of the culture
through a radical new growth or maturation process. His
Freudian interpretation of history sees all present civilization as the product of repression leading inevitably to destruction. His novel interpretation of the doctrine of the
resurrection of the body lies in terms of overcoming man's
alienation from his own physical body through a return to
the pleasure principle and polymorphous play of early
childhood.

But Herbert Marcuse' revolution is to be carried out not in the name of the id but of Reason. His criteria for evaluating the positive social change that he seeks, however when explored, are rather vague. In proposing the criteria for the truth value of different historical projects, Marcuse lists the following: "(1) The transcendent project must be in accordance with the real possibilities open at the attained level of the material and intellectual culture. (2) The transcendent project, in order to falsify the established totality, must demonstrate its own *higher* rationality in the threefold sense that (a) it offers the prospect of preserving and improving the productive achievements of civilization; (b) it defines the established totality in its very structure, basic tendencies, and relations; (c) its realization offers a greater chance for the pacification of existence, within the framework of institutions which offer a greater chance for the free development of human needs and faculties."[32] Even his definition of pacification and "free" development of human needs and faculties is unclear. He writes: "These concepts can be empirically defined in terms of the available intellectual and material resources and capabilities and their systematic use for attenuating the struggle for existence. This is the objective ground of historical rationality."[33] But, of course, one might say that Tillich's trust in the outcome of the Kairos represented by the social crisis of our era with the possibility of the new theonomy, is also a vague conception. Both Tillich and Marcuse are in agreement in expressing confidence in reason defined much more broadly than simply technological reason as capable of providing answers to the crises of our time.[34] "Civilization produces the means for freeing Nature from its own brutality, its own insufficiency, its own blindness, by virtue of the cognitive and transforming power of Reason. And Reason can fulfill this function only as post-technological rationality, in which technics is itself the instrumentality of pacification, organon of the 'art of life.' The function of Reason then converges with the function of

Art."[35.] However, Marcuse would appear to be more utopian than Tillich. This is reflected in his assumption that
the man who knows the truth will follow it.[36] "Inasmuch as
the struggle for truth 'saves' reality from destruction, truth
commits and engages human existence. It is the essentially
human project. If man has learned to see and know what
really *is*, he will act in accordance with truth. Epistemology is in itself ethics, and ethics is epistemology."[37] Marcuse lacks the restraining influence that the conception of
sin provides Tillich. Marcuse also appears to be prepared
to exercise more direct political restraint upon those who
disagree with him than Tillich would have been willing
to do. Marcuse' philosophy lacks Tillich's awareness of
the demonic which expresses itself in even the most creative of human endeavors. And, his new atheistic system is
totally devoid of the sense of eschatological transcendence
beyond any possible historical achievements. Perhaps it is
what theologians might term his naïve optimism that makes
Marcuse so attractive to student idealists.

While both writers—each within his own system—point
to the necessity of personal renewal as well as the renewal
of external society, Tillich places a much greater emphasis upon this process. The power of the New Being for
Tillich is not only found in political movements but is ap-
prehended by the individual in the personal experiences
of his life. This also may account for Tillich's not being
as popular with some young people as Marcuse, for many
of the activists, seeing the need for change in society, are
somewhat reluctant to see the need for change in themselves.[38] Thus despite many similarities between their
positions, there are major differences between Tillich and
Marcuse. They center on Tillich's commitment to a theistic position that trusts in a power which transcends nature
to break through and express itself in new forms. The same
theism, however, rejects any utopian attempts to achieve
perfection in society because of the presence of the demonic and the experience of original sin. Curiously enough,

despite his utopianism, Marcuse also seems to be increasingly more pessimistic about the possibility of any real change because he maintains so much power resides in the hands of those who benefit from the things as they are in technological societies.

We have seen that what lies behind a great deal of student unrest and what undergirds the thought of many "aware" student activists is the awareness of a seeming tension between direct experience of the world (intuitive-aesthetic) and the objective distancing experience (detached-scientific). Objectivity is identified with science and through science with all education. The argument is that conflict between these two positions has pried apart thinking and feeling, reason and passion, opinion and conviction. But it is our contention that they belong together. Only a caricature of "science" or "art" holds them apart. Nonetheless, popular impressions and usage support this caricature. It is instructive to remember that there is no term in English that expresses the unity of thought and feeling. Tillich has to use the German *Geist* and Marcuse "Reason" to attempt to identify those elements which together make up the knowledge process—reason, passion, conviction, decision, and creativity.

As the college and university curricula have increasingly fallen under the influences of a narrowly conceived science, the impression has been given that knowledge is inimical to feeling and objectivity is to be preferred over immediacy of experience. The social sciences and even the humanities have fallen under the influence of this view insofar as they have sought to justify themselves by mimicking the natural sciences. Thus in the minds of many students, the university, its colleges and departments, have sold themselves, cheaply, to be in the service of science. This is a particularly vexatious problem for the liberal arts college within the major university because of the dominant influence of the graduate and professional schools that surround it. It has been observed that graduate education in our time is particularly sterile. Many of the requirements for the doctoral degree demand not increased sensitivity to major problems but becoming expert in some detached subject matter. The requirement that a dissertation be a unique contribution to learning itself forces the candidate to place attention upon trivia that no one else has bothered to explore.

The problem facing colleges and universities is therefore the problem of major change in order to heal the apparent breach between thinking and feeling, opinion and commitment, facts and convictions. Radical change must come and if it is true that youth are not always intelligent about how it should come, they are at least emotionally aware that come it will. Those institutions in which youth make their most important decisions (regarding vocation, political orientation, life philosophy or commitment, and life mate) must themselves change in order to provide guidance for those who will continue to direct change within the wider society. Thus the decisive issue facing colleges is whether they will be obstacles to change or provide the necessary resources for making the great social changes that will occur in the last half of the twentieth century—making them intelligently and in continuity with the evolution of the democratic achievement of the past.

A decisive role in answering this question belongs in a real sense to the faculty—those within the college and university who possess access to the resources of wisdom and perspective which must be shared with students who in increasing numbers are emotionally for change but have not subjected themselves to disciplines that can bring it about. But, as we have noted, faculty may have a built-in disposition for detachment. This attitudinal factor, however, has been in many cases surmounted, particularly when faculty come to be valued for this novel type of social contribution. But the most difficult task for faculty is still the challenge given by Professor Arrowsmith—the willingness to be models for their students. If students find that the academic discipline that faculty have undergone has enabled them to be more effective change agents and has increased the options for decisions as well as enriched the lives of faculty, then they may well be willing to undergo similar discipline themselves. This can only happen if there is close and frequent contact between students and faculty. But the curriculum also must afford opportunity for expressing the affirmation that reflection and discipline do affect positively the quality of experience. This means that despite possible objection from the departments more issue-centered curricula must be developed not merely because the issues appear to be relevant to the students (a most unsure and changing basis upon which to build a curriculum) but because issues provide the opportunity for involvement in decision-making—an experience students sorely miss in most present higher education. Thus, something like a balance must be restored between the library-classroom and experience in the key places of decision-making in college and society. But this means that the college must take upon itself wholly new tasks. It may even be that these tasks are beyond the possibility of achievement. But in any case they must be explored and examined.

5

The "Impossible" Role
of the Liberal Arts Colleges

IN WESTERN SOCIETIES the exploration of the questions of man's nature and what is of highest value has not been confined to nor been the exclusive property of religious institutions. The exploration of these questions has also centered in that product of religious organizations—the liberal arts college. After the inculcation of the young in the history and value patterns of the parent society (what traditionally has been known as paideia), a task carried on in grade and high school, but before the teaching of the specific vocational skills necessary for the operation of a complex society (techne), there has traditionally been a period of time set aside for the broadening of perspectives and the exploration of questions of ultimate value. It is true that the focus of emphasis in the liberal arts college has, until very recently, been almost exclusively upon Western culture. But making allowances for this narrow focus, it must be admitted that the concern was to break through the parochialism of the particular national culture and open up broader vistas through exposure to the accumulated wisdom of mankind.[39] Hence the concern for foreign languages—originally Latin as the tongue which introduced scholars into the dialogue of the universal company of scholars and later the various vernaculars as avenues to different cultural perspectives and achievements.

The particular history and peculiar needs of American society influenced the unique development of the liberal arts college within the Western hemisphere. Here swiftly increasing wealth provided for the possibility of a longer period of general education before the pressure for vocational training made itself felt. Also, this society, lacking an established aristocracy or long traditions of civil service, needed to educate an unprecedented percentage of the total population if the experiment in democratic living were to succeed. Founded generally under ecclesiastical sponsorship, the liberal arts college performed two functions that reflect this inherited view of higher education. First, through a study of history, religion, philosophy, and literature, it traced for its students the principal achievements of Western man—interpreted, of course, within the fundamental framework of the commitments of those sponsoring the college. Secondly, college instruction provided a foundation through the study of mathematics and the natural and social sciences for the professional and vocational training to follow. Behind this pattern there lay the presupposition that a vocation was indeed a genuine "calling," that is, a commitment to which young people would give themselves and through which it was hoped and presumed they would also discover their identity.

There are today, however, a number of factors that seriously modify, if not completely inhibit, these functions from being carried on within the present educational milieu. First among these are the excessive claims being made by the vocational aspects of education. Certainly the goal of a very high percentage of the large number of young people seeking a college education since World War II has been to "learn a better living." College students no longer comprise an "elect." They are not the selected few who can afford the luxury of studying the eternal verities before settling down to the practical business of earning a living. The needs of business, industry, and government for technically trained specialists has eventuated in pressures for early identification of majors within the disciplines. And the grave problems facing general education everywhere attest to the difficulty colleges are having in retaining anything like the traditional broad cultural foundations. Furthermore, the vastly increased cost of science laboratories has meant that the time and attention of administrators has been given more and more to providing for the efficient use of this constantly dated equipment. Not enough energy has been devoted to keeping the humanities in an equivalent state of good repair.

A very large percentage of liberal arts colleges also face the problem that their location (generally at a distance from major metropolitan centers) removes them from "where the action is." These colleges were established and flourished in a small-town atmosphere which was once ideally suited to the perceived tasks of unhurried contemplation of the long annals of cultural growth and achievement. But as the curriculum now moves more and more in the direction of being issue centered, these colleges find that their geographic locations are hindrances rather than a help. Large numbers of colleges now have "overseas programs" in Europe and, increasingly, even within the underdeveloped countries of Africa, Latin America, and Asia. A few of them are so aware of this problem that they are joining forces with other colleges to establish urban program consortia so that they may conduct metropolitan semesters for their students in nearby population centers. It is doubtful whether many of those conducting such experiments are aware of the full implications to their total life and curricula of this setting up of a mixture of study, observation, and involvement courses.

The liberal arts college within the university has generally been more favorably located than has the small independent or church-related college. This is because most major universities are either in or very close to large cities. But the problem is by no means resolved merely by the fortune of geographical propinquity. As has been observed, the liberal arts college in the university labors under the difficulty of having to compete with other areas of the university for funds. And it has grave difficulty in attempting to provide quality undergraduate education when so much time, attention, and concern is funneled into the more glamorous graduate and vocational programs.

Nevertheless, the key decisions affecting the future of liberal arts education must take place in these university-based colleges. They may occur within some of the select cluster colleges and a few particularly strong independent ones as well. This will be the case for no other reason than that the small independent schools face an increasingly bleak financial future. That reforms will primarily be in the university-based colleges also reflects the fact that advantages may be found in geographic location as well as in the potential of relationship with specific kinds of graduate programs. Liberal arts colleges must give high priority to the reexamination and careful delineation of their unique functions. They must be something more than a stage between high school and vocational work, a kind of entertaining, marking step for students while waiting to get into graduate school.

It is curious that the traditional functions of a liberal arts education should be lost sight of by many within the colleges just at a time when the mood and ethos of the student generation cries out for an opportunity to explore the very issues that have traditionally been dominant in higher education. That students should feel they must move outside the liberal arts college to establish experimental colleges and "free universities" to deal with the problems of identity, meaning, value, and morality underscores the bankruptcy of much liberal arts education as it is being carried on today. The concern dominating so much of the leadership within the liberal arts—the emphasis upon providing the basis for later specialization within the various disciplines—has to be balanced by a responsible return to more "generalist" concerns.

It may be helpful in comprehending what is an appeal for a return to a past although updated conception of liberal arts education to look briefly at some aspects of the history of the development of the college and university. This tracing of a particular set of themes will indicate some present values that derive from past higher education. It hopefully will demonstrate as well the novelty of the situation that liberal arts education currently faces. What is being called for is certainly no slavish return to a bygone set of patterns but a fresh adaptation to meet current needs and opportunities.

In the correspondence between Pope Gregory XII and John Gerson, one of the early rectors of the University of Paris, reference is found to a startlingly creative conception of the university. The form in which this idea is expressed clearly shows the influence of both the Hellenistic and Hebraic cultural strains that were coming together so fruitfully in the developing medieval culture. It is curious that this medieval conception only now has the possibility of becoming a practical reality. The idea expressed was that the health of Christendom depended upon the balanced expression of three coordinate centers of power. Cast in terms of a traditional theology, the idea was that the three roles of Christ—Prophet, Priest, and King—each were represented by a special institution within Christian society. The whole society was conceived to be an expression of the Second Person of the Trinity whose destiny according to Scripture was to be him who fills all things and in whom all things hold together (Col. 1:17). The kingly rule of Christ was said to be expressed by the functioning of the state. The earthly monarch was the vicegerent of God. The church, of course, carried on the priestly function of representing God and his purposes to man and interceding before God on behalf of men. But it was to the infant institution, the university, that these medieval writers assigned the prophetic or critical role.[40] Thus the probing, questioning function expressed in the Socratic heritage received fresh impetus as, in the founding of Western universities, it was augmented by the prophetic tradition which is traced back a century earlier than Plato.

Regardless of the truth of the theology it reflected, this conception of the university as the institution called upon to exercise a critical function within society was one which profoundly influenced the whole nature of higher education. This idea is seen in the special prerogatives of the medieval college or university, existing as it did in walled isolation from the town, and may be reflected in its relative freedom from governmental and church control.[41] Implicit in this conception is the idea that higher education does not consist merely in the acquisition of facts or information but in the development of a critical intelligence capable of exercising independent judgment. But fruitful as this idea was, there were major problems from its very inception. Gregory's idea logically entailed that the three institutions, government, religion, and university, should be of sufficiently equal power that one was not under the domination of the others. Actually, in the mind of Gregory whose high view of the papacy was the foundation of later claims to almost total authority, the church, as dispenser of grace and guardian of revelation, was the primary institution whose will state and university were bound to obey. The fact is that colleges and universities were never independent centers of criticism in either Catholic or Protestant countries. In fact, they remained under ecclesiastical patronage and control until the beginning of this century. Then with the initiation of state-supported higher education the university began to exchange ecclesiastical control for governmental. Of course, in enlightened nations both church and government respected a carefully exercised academic freedom including the judicious use of the right to criticize, which has become the hallmark of all higher learning as opposed to mere indoctrination. Yet neither college nor university was free to develop into what it might have been in Gregory's vision. That possibility is only now being explored as the society of the near future will increasingly recognize the university as the primary means of its health and development. The final realization of the medieval vision would also necessitate a solution to the not insoluble problem of seeing to it that the financial contributions of government and industry would not entail any untoward pressure upon institutions of higher learning.[42] But the danger must be recognized that colleges and universities which at long last have escaped from ecclesiastical control may fall almost completely under government control. This is one of the strongest arguments for the need to continue private, independent institutions of higher learning.

Activist students are forcing a confrontation on the issue of why colleges and universities are so dependent upon the establishment. They criticize the colleges and universities for accepting the role of producing people who will "fit into" things as they are. But the problem that is particularly faced by the liberal arts college is not just that of asserting its freedom from state, ecclesiastical, or establishment control in order that it might render the idea of critical service. Changes within society have altered the role of other institutions, particularly the church, the family, and government so that entirely new conditions must be faced by the colleges. Profound changes in the parent culture produced by the development of technology are forcing upon the colleges and universities entirely new functions which they have never performed before or which they have performed in very different ways.

One of the most commented upon characteristics of the present era is its pervasive secularism. The process of de-sacralizing the world which Paul Tillich reminds us was stimulated by the Hebrew prophets, by Greek philosophy, and by Reformation piety, has affected every area of human life and every institution in Western society including the church. It really does not matter what are regarded as the decisive factors in making for this triumph of the secular—whether it be the influence of the Judeo-Christian tradition, as Harvey Cox would indicate, or the removal of any locus for the sacred by the invention of printing (which divided

up space into uniform, repeatable units) as Marshall
McLuhan claims. The fact is that for this college generation
the pervasive secularism means that the church no longer
functions as the guarantor of ultimate meaning or the pro-
vider of the value patterns of civilization.

Young people, as Herbert Marcuse deplores, tend to
think in terms of images more than in terms of concepts.
This is one of the fruits of the technological era and its
reproductive organ—advertising. Concepts are more
explicit than images but they are less vivid. And the
images that young people have of the church reflect the
triumph of the desacralizing process. There are three
primary images evoked by institutional religion in the
minds of many thoughtful young people. The first image is
that of the corporation. The medieval guild both imitated
and shaped the structures of the church in that time, so
the dominant organizational form of our age—the business
corporation—molds the structures of institutional religion
today. The criteria of success for the church seems to be the
same as those for any business corporation. The church is
measured by statistics and judged by the size of buildings
and the number of clientele. There is little awareness of
the conception of the Biblical image of the church as the
body of Christ, which like Jesus' body, must be broken for
the life of the world. This means that the growth pattern of
the church's life is viewed as that of the expanding corporation rather than the rhythm of death and resurrection.
Those few who are theologically sophisticated would give
assent to the proposition that the question that ought to be
asked by those who are responsible for the organizational
life of the church should not be, How can we keep the
church from dying? but, How can the church die in such a
way that it might be raised in newness of life? But even
among this theological elite there is concern and dismay at
the recent leveling off of church attendance and the down-
turn in all other indicators of church influence.[43] For young
people religion is big business.

The second image of the church held by increasing numbers of young people is that it is the conservator of past values of society. There is, of course, no crime in conserving what is of value. But the image that the church has is that of a museum of middle-class values. The church's incapacity to hold on to any influence with the working class and its increasing irrelevance to the growing affluent class are both indications that what the church really celebrates and enshrines are chiefly the values of the increasingly out-of-date work-oriented middle class. The Biblical image of the church as a priestly fellowship, that is, one which represents man to God and therefore celebrates solidarity with the world is not dramatically evident. Where it is, this image is severely damaged by the manifest dissent of most laymen from those costly forms of priestly action which some denominations have undertaken in the racial crisis, in concern for migrant workers, and in the antipoverty campaign.

The third image of the church is held not only by young people but by a large segment of the total population. This is the image of the convenient service center. The church is conceived of as an easily accessible organization which provides the locus for a host of social functions from Boy Scout troops to Golden Age clubs. Now of all the popularly held images of the church, this one has most to be said for it. Not only has service (*diakonia*) had a long and honorable tradition within the church, but out of it may come such possibly fruitful conceptions as the church functioning as a kind of convener of society. Ideally the church could provide a locus in which various competing groups could come together for dialogue and cooperative action. This role for the church would have great potential if the identification of the church with the particular concerns of the middle class could be overcome.[44] But the fact that perhaps the most acceptable image of the church today is that of a social service center indicates the extent of the process of secularization. Any number of organizations in society perform social services. This image would therefore put the church alongside neighborhood houses, hospitals, clinics, the Peace Corps, and even the college as organizations dedicated to various forms of social service within the community.

Where these images have a particular bearing on the role of the liberal arts college is that in none of them does the church fulfill the function of providing the basic meaning structures which hold society together. In our time the performance of that function falls more and more to the liberal arts college. Instead of being able to rely upon a comparatively homogeneous set of meanings and values conceived as originating in God and communicated to all segments of society by the missionary and nurturing functions of the church, the college and university today are faced with a totally new situation. They are finding themselves called upon to provide for the coming generation what the church traditionally has given. And the fact is that the college is almost totally unprepared for this new assignment. And there are certain conditions within the college and particularly within some of its disciplines which mitigate against the easy assumption of this new role.

We have already noted that many faculty are uncomfortable in being treated as models or moral preceptors, let alone performing pastoral tasks for students. The size of many colleges and universities also precludes a too close association between faculty and students and therefore hampers the performance of this function. Ultimate meanings and personal values are more often transmitted through informal association than through classroom experiences.[45] The criteria for promotion of faculty and for their monetary reward as well as advancement within their own disciplines places obstacles before the faculty member who might desire to contribute to this new ecclesiastical function of liberal arts education. The lack of any truly academic community in most colleges and universities further increases the problem. Development of the cluster-college concept and the springing up of many new smaller residence units which also act as instructional units may provide some resources to meet this particular problem.

Then, too, until comparatively recently, most universities and colleges did not have formal courses in religion. Where they existed, their identification with the sponsoring denominations made them suspect as an attempt at indoctrinating students with the point of view of the ecclesiastical establishment. At the same time philosophy, which might have capitalized upon the new quest for values in a secular age, had to a great extent eschewed all metaphysical and value questions in order to concentrate on linguistic analysis in the service of science.[46] Thus the colleges have not been equipped to shoulder a new burden that a secular generation of students places upon it. Students have increasingly felt the need to go outside the formal educational structures by setting up experimental colleges in order to find answers to this "religious" quest.

The situation may be described in terms of an increasing tide of secularism thrusting the priestly function on top of the critical function traditionally performed by colleges and universities. It may safely be predicted that future college generations, increasingly deprived or not willing to avail themselves of religious instruction, will expect higher education to provide them with answers to fundamental meaning questions. These questions are not, as we have seen, foreign to the basic aims of a college education. The twin questions of the nature and destiny of man and what is of highest value are, as we have said, religious issues. But the modern college and university have to a great extent forgotten this fact. And what has really proven to be the stumbling block is that the colleges are not committed to fulfilling this role. For the most part they appear to be hesitant to undertake the restructuring and transformation of values which this new task requires. Educators have been reluctant to face up to the new situation occasioned by the church's loss of its position as moral tutor of society.

Educators are even embarrassed in facing the question of the nature of truth and what it is they are attempting to communicate. There is an irony that the question which must now be faced by colleges in the latter half of the twentieth century is the not unfamiliar question, Can virtue be taught?[47]

We are prophesying that, as higher education ceases to be merely a four-to-seven-year phenomenon but becomes a regular component in adult life, institutions of higher learning must more and more function to provide what the church in the past provided—the meaning system and the value pattern by which society functions. But the problem of the colleges does not stop with their having to face the taking up of traditionally ecclesiastical roles. There is a sense in which the third of Pope Gregory's coordinate powers also has to be faced by the college and in somewhat different manner than it has in the past. The college has performed a long-established and well-recognized task of preparing people trained to serve within government. In addition to preparing to staff the professions of law, medicine, and the ministry, most colleges saw themselves as equipping students for political tasks which, in an oligarchic society, were the particular responsibilities of the educated elite. With the advent of popular democracy and a vast increase in numbers of students attending college, this political task was modified. Not only were young people to be trained for service within government but also as citizens they needed a foundation in politics in order to exercise their responsibilities. Thus American colleges and universities undertook what was a new function, at least in scope, though it was but the extension of an older recognized one—education for political responsibility.

Today this political function of the colleges and universities is being radically shaken by the activist student generation. At a time in which politics is of increasing importance and plagued with unprecedented numbers of problems, the colleges are turned to on every hand for answers to political questions. For many professional politicians and for a growing number of private citizens, the vexatious nature of the contemporary political situation makes educational institutions take on a role of potential savior of society. "After all," they say, "aren't the colleges supposed to be problem-solving institutions?" Thus we find faculty members consulted by government on a host of problems to a degree unknown in the past. But we also see students scrutinized to see if they are manifesting the high degree of political responsibility that is deemed desirable in an era of change. There is a sad ambivalence about the adult response to the student political activism. Although adults appear pleased that students are concerned about politics, they are alarmed that student politics is not just a carbon copy of established political patterns.

The new political role of the college and university is partly responsible for the widespread reaction of student protest. Any examination of the history of the college or university, not merely in South America but in Europe and America as well, will show that college campuses have been far from islands of tranquillity where issues of eternal verity have been abstractly considered. The time-honored "town and gown warfare" was often characterized by incidents far less worthy of serious consideration than those which have motivated many of the student activists today such as racial prejudice, war, social injustice. But when a campus is torn by debate, dissension, and protest, there is general public indignation on every hand. This is because, in the public mind, the college and university should now provide a model for quiet civil conduct. This means that, to some extent, the college is expected to fulfill a kingly as well as a priestly and prophetic function.

Colleges and universities cannot escape the challenge of providing training in politics. But they can only do so by becoming the nexus in which political issues, those internal to the college, and external to it, as well as national and international issues, are expressed with the full range of their attendant passions. What is more, they are called upon to relate political issues to the fundamental meaning questions of our time.[48]

There is another institution whose functions the college is called upon to fulfill in new ways in our time. This is the parental function of the family. At a time when family structure is more loosely knit than ever before—when the identity crisis is exacerbated by the lack of any clear male and female roles traditionally communicated by parents—and in a time known for its wide generation gap, many college students are unconsciously looking to faculty and college administrators as parental surrogates. Many of the most brilliant students seek to increase the depth of their contact with faculty members because they lack a close relation to their parents. And they resent much more than many faculty (who are used to the system) the publish or perish edicts of administrators or reduced teaching loads being given as rewards to professors. It may not be fanciful to speculate that one of the factors that has made the *in loco parentis* debate so important for contemporary students is just that, in the students' minds, this is what the colleges have become—the only parents he knows. And what he resents most is that this parent surrogate endeavors to treat him like an immature child rather than a maturing adult. The fact is that most students do want to have their colleges or universities take a personal interest in them. Some students may cite with approval the model of the European universities with their total disregard of the students' extracurricular life. But what they are really protesting are rules that reflect a double standard, an unrealistic and condescending set of rules in the formulation of which they have had no part. When the criteria for evaluating student life becomes that which effectively contributes to the enrichment of the total educational experience and when students have a say in what these experiences are, they generally respond favorably to the college concern to regulate the quality of campus life. And as we have said, every study confirms the vital importance of the co-curriculum as being far more important than the formal curriculum in terms of long-range influence upon the student. Colleges and universities should not try to find a simple way out of the dilemma by shunning what society and many of their best students are asking them to do.

We have seen that the college has fallen heir not only to the traditional educational task but to religious, political, and moral tasks as well. It might well be asked whether this accretion of priestly, governmental, and parental roles is not placing too much of a burden upon any one institution in our society. Whether ideally the college should be called upon to deal with all the major functions of a civilized society is a reasonable question. But however this question is answered, it will not alter the facts. For better or worse the college is now freighted with these unprecedented expectations.[49]

As we have stated, none of the new roles the colleges are challenged with is totally foreign to what the college has been or the role it did perform in varying degrees in the past. There are old and new resources available to the colleges and universities to help them meet the rising tide of student and community expectations. But educators, though sometimes flattered by the prominence of their new roles within society, are more often alarmed at the magnitude of the demands that are being placed upon them, especially since they regard the institution they serve to be already overburdened.

Radical changes will be needed if the colleges and universities are to be creative in responding to these radical new conditions. A clarity of conception as to what their primary tasks are is being forced upon faculty and administrators. The colleges will have to become more sharply defined in their functions at the same time that they are becoming more loosely knit in their structures. They must overcome the rigidities imposed upon them by their inherited departmental divisions and provide more issue-centered curricula and new ways of helping to shape the co-curriculum. The possibility of these things happening depends to a major degree upon cooperation among students, faculty, and administrators. A major change in Western culture once took place because of a reformation instigated by professors. The sixteenth-century Protestant Reformation is sometimes referred to as the "magisterial reformation," because it was begun by professors. What is desperately needed in the secular church, that is, the liberal arts college, today is a new reformation. Whether such a second magisterial reformation will take place is questionable. The possibilities may best be explored from within the context of looking at the history of the three major reformations that have transformed and are transforming Western religion.

6

Three Concurrent Reformations: Another Revolt of the Magisters

ALTHOUGH there is little general recognition of it today because of its classification either as an event in church history or, paradoxically, as part of a general social and political movement, the Protestant Reformation originated as an academic movement. Many of the precursors of the sixteenth-century Reformers, such as John Hus and John Wycliffe, were university professors while Calvin, Luther, and Bucer were all academicians.[50] The recognized dependence of the Reformation upon Renaissance studies should serve to remind us of the pervasive academic ethos of this protest movement. And their horrified rejection of the Anabaptist movement with its peasant base betrays their elitist position as members of a privileged intelligentsia.

It is more widely recognized that one of the immediate impacts of the Reformation within the general society was an increase in the concern for education. With its emphasis upon the need for every man to read the Scripture and its concern for complex theological issues, Protestantism required a literate following.[51] Prof. George Williams has meticulously demonstrated not only the pervasive religious motivation but also the fascinating continuity of what he terms a wilderness-paradise theme which lay behind the establishment of colleges in the New World. Williams shows how the concept of a college—with its walled campus—was regarded as the reestablishment of a Garden of Eden in the midst of a chaotic world.

A closer analysis of the magisterial reformation and its roots indicates that the very concept of reformation is an indigenous one within the institutions of the Judeo-Christian tradition and that this reformation idea overflows into the cultures in which these institutions exist and upon which they have exerted great influence. The theme of change and reform is a reflection of a particular kind of religion, one which has been classified as "historical," that is, one which finds the dominant focus of its concern in the fluctuating historical milieu as over against what may be termed "nature" religions, those which focus primarily upon the stability and regularity of the sequential natural order. The Jewish and Christian Scriptures express a predilection to accept change, especially when it is understood in terms of reform and, in particular, the prophetic tradition which they share gives impetus to the acceptance of reformations within these religions. This pattern may be seen clearly within Judaism alone. This religious tradition experienced a Deuteronomic reformation, a profound change during the Babylonic captivity, the development of Rabbinic Judaism, widespread influence from the Hasidic movement, and the evolution of Reformed Judaism in America.

The German theologian Hans-Ruedi Weber has identified within Christianity what he terms an "Israel element" and a "Christ event element" in constant dialectical relationship. Included within the Israel element are the characteristics of continuity, identity, and conservation, and within the Christ event element the features of criticism, discontinuity, and radical change.[52]

Indeed, the whole history of Christianity may be seen as a series of great reformations. The first of these took place in the early centuries of the common era. This was a reformation that transformed Christianity from being a sect within Judaism into a world religion. A second reformation took place in the sixteenth century which transformed Christianity, at least in theory, from being merely one side of a culture that was divided into a sacred and a secular realm. This reformation involved an attempt to destroy the division that the medieval world had accepted between the secular and the sacred: the church's area and the world's area. Today we are living in the midst of what may be called the third great reformation of Christianity. This is one moving to transform Christianity from being just another human religion into a way of living in the world. Its apparent goals are the transformation of Christianity from allegiance to particular ecclesiastical and doctrinal commitments to a style of life, one that would not be termed religious but secular. The radical nature of this transformation can be seen in its view that faith is not that which prepares one for the afterlife but provides resources for living in the present changing world. It is thus a reflection of that general movement from a transcendent to an immanent orientation which we indicated as characterizing the ethos of our time.

Each of these three great reformations represents a movement that has extended the implications of the original Christian faith, going beyond the previously regarded limits of the interpretation of the gospel. Each of these reformations, therefore, has involved a change in the expression and meaning of what was said to be the vital core of the New Testament. Each movement has involved the working out of what the reformers claimed to be implicit in the gospel but which was up to their time not yet identified or had not yet become relevant or explicit. Behind each of these major reformations there was also a charismatic leader who identified the central issue of the reformation although subsequent events generally have gone beyond his insights. Each reformation also produced an extremist group that has taken some of the ideas of the charismatic leader and pushed them to such an extreme that it has occasioned reaction within the reformation itself. Thus we find that a reformation is much more complex than simply an expression of the opposition between certain would-be reformers and those who refuse to be reformed; there has always been extremely lively debate and radical dissension within the camp of the reformers themselves. Also, it should be observed, each of these reformations has eventually had to come to some kind of terms with that against which it originally protested. That is to say, each reformation has had to progress to the point of being able to see that what was being protested against also had some validity. Thus something like a synthesis between two positions was finally accepted.

A brief review of these past reformations will indicate that they have elements about them which should have interest for more than church historians. Even the first two reformations we have identified are significant today because their key issues are still operative, at least in the life of religious organizations in our time, and it may be argued in institutions of higher learning as well. An understanding of these reformations, all having their genesis in the past but still operating today, may assist in comprehending something of the traumatic time in which religious institutions exist today and the even more stormy years into which most institutions of society are moving.

The first century saw what could be called the "catholic" reformation of the nascent Christian faith. Under the dynamic leadership of the apostle Paul, Christianity ceased to be merely a sect within the minor religion of Judaism and became a missionary and finally a world faith. It was the mission to the Gentile world, the peculiar contribution of Paul, that produced a reformation or revolution within early Christianity. Paul rejected the thesis, accepted by Peter and the other apostles, that Christianity was an improved or fulfilled Judaism and that converts had to become Jews before they became Christians. This is what the whole circumcision issue in the New Testament is about. But, according to Paul, what distinguished Christians from Jews was not merely that they had added to Judaism the affirmation that Jesus was the expected Messiah. Paul rather vastly reshaped Christianity by claiming that faith in the gospel annulled legalistic Judaism. The New Testament gives evidence of the very stormy debate that took place on this question at the end of which Paul won the freedom to maintain his interpretation of Christianity in his mission to the Gentiles. Because of the failure of Christianity to attract a major Jewish following and the circumstances of the first and second Jewish wars, it was Paul's originally minor expression of Christianity that became the dominant and finally orthodox position. Because of historic events that ensured the success of the Gentile mission, Christianity therefore became primarily a Gentile religion. What is more, the Gentile Christianity came into creative relationship with Greek philosophy, Roman law and organization. Thus a new phenomenon developed which we had occasion to mention a number of times. What eventuated was what is known as Christendom, a catholic, world faith that changed the face of the earth and the course of human history.

As we have noted, the key theological issue for Paul was the relationship between the law and the gospel. Did one have to become a Jew first and accept the law and then add the gospel on top of the law so that the law was the fundamental affirmation and the gospel was something added on top of that? As a Pharisee, Paul had been reared in the religion of law, but he came to the conclusion that the gospel was primary and in a very real sense it annulled the law. As it has been expressed, Paul affirmed that God's initiative, his indicative, preceded his imperative and that this was true from the very beginning. God's liberating activity (the gospel), the good news of God acting to free his people, was regarded as a more fundamental insight into his nature than the command or demand that the law laid upon man. Even the Ten Commandments begin not with the imperative but with the indicative "I am the Lord thy God, which have brought thee out of the land of Egypt, out of the house of bondage." From this came an understanding of God as committed to human freedom. This, contemporary radical theology would argue, is the foundation for his preeminence over other gods. Commandment is said to be built upon gospel. Thus Paul constantly preached the freedom of the Christian from basing his faith upon law. But there were many who heard Paul's preaching and who carried his conception of freedom to an extreme that Paul never anticipated. These were the so-called "antinomians" who taught that Christians, freed from the law, could do anything they wanted to. They apparently even advocated that one might sin more so that grace might more abound. These antinomians found in Christianity a stimulating faith which permitted them to do anything they pleased. So we find Paul constantly rebuking what he regards to be a malicious misinterpretation of his position.

But the victorious Pauline expression of Christianity, with its ambiguous understanding of the place of law, left Christians with very deep unresolved problems. There was the problem with which even Paul had to deal of the regulation of the life of the Christian within the world. Paul's claim that the law was the occasion for sin, almost verging upon sin itself, left much of Christianity without clear guidelines as to ethical behavior, let alone a system of social regulations. There was also the very pressing problem of the relationship between the Christians and Jews. Judaism proved to be a faith that just refused to die out by conversion of its adherents. Indeed, a basic issue in contemporary Jewish-Christian relationships is a necessity of continuing the discussion regarding law and gospel which was begun by Paul. Christians today are exploring the meaning of the continued existence of Israel as the people of God, and Jews and Christians together are being forced to reexamine the need for a relationship between their insights, hopefully coming up with a position that does not eventuate in a cold legalism on the one side or in moral license on the other. Thus the issue that was initiated in the first great catholic reformation of Christianity remains unresolved today.

A brief examination of the Protestant Reformation of the sixteenth century will suffice for our purposes. This is because it is the reform movement with which most people are best acquainted. It is agreed that this reformation took up the law-gospel controversy of the first catholic reformation but expressed it in terms of the relationship between faith and good works. Luther saw clearly the implication of Paul's affirmation that God's salvation was a free gift, independent of any merit on the part of man and to be accepted by faith alone. Thus Luther added the word *sola* (alone) to Paul's Epistle to the Romans in order to make this crystal clear: according to Luther, faith alone made a man whole. But the implications of Luther's teaching of justification by faith had a tremendous impact on the nature of the church as an institution. The power of the church as a monolithic structure was broken, for it was not the church that saved man but the individual's faith within the church. The result was that Christians were liberated from bondage to an all-embracing, hierarchic, exclusive channel of grace. The church ceased to be the most important institution in the life of Western man.

There were those who took these basic ideas of Paul and Luther and carried them to what the reformers felt was an unjustifiable extreme. Shortly after Luther's breach with Rome, Lutherans and Calvinists found themselves pitted against the Anabaptists who scorned all rules, all structures, all customs. Thus there was a great deal of dissent within the reformers' camp as Reformed and Lutheran Christians condemned the excesses of Anabaptist revolutionaries. What is more, Protestantism began to display its tendency to divisiveness as the Lutheran, Reformed, and Anglican churches, which came out of the sixteenth-century Reformation, each produced different answers to the question of how the church should be organized. Although the roots of the Protestant denominations in America lie within the sixteenth-century formulations, these answers are not really relevant to the situation facing the church today. In the secular age Christian witness is blunted by divisions within Christendom that seem to have only an antiquarian interest. What is more, Protestant individualism has placed an extraordinarily heavy burden of personal responsibility upon the believers which they seem increasingly unwilling or unable to bear. Then, too, there is the factor of continuing Roman Catholicism. Like Judaism, it did not die or just go away. Now Protestants and Catholics find themselves engaging in a dialogue that has never occurred before in their history. Protestants are pondering the meaning of the continued existence of Roman Catholicism and vice versa. And both sides are beginning to explore the nature and kind of personal freedom a Christian has as a believer and, at the same time, what kind of an institutional structure should exist to express that freedom.

It has been claimed that we are at present in the midst of the third great reformation. The present one appears to be as pervasive in its implications as the previous reformations at which we looked very briefly. The question raised by the present reformation is whether Christianity can be restructured on another basis than being just one of man's many religions. This is the issue of the possibility of what is called "religionless Christianity." This is, of course, the phrase of the German martyr Dietrich Bonhoeffer. Despite the brevity of his career, brought to an untimely close by his execution at the hands of the Nazis, he appears to be the charismatic leader who has given impetus to this third reformation. Just because we are at present living in the midst of this reformation we cannot be as clear about its general outlines and directions as we can about the other two reformations from which, in their initiation at least, we are separated by a helpful distance in time.

However, it is possible to identify a few of the features of the present reformation. If the problem for Paul was the meaning of the gospel to a pagan-gentile world and the problem for Luther was the meaning of the gospel to a world dominated by the church, then it might be said that the modern problem, with which Bonhoeffer wrestled, is the meaning of the gospel for a secular world. To use another of Bonhoeffer's famous phrases, what does Christian faith mean to a "world come of age"? How does a Christian react to a world that no longer turns to holy mother church to find answers to its pressing problems? The issue is whether traditional religion has anything to say to a world that acts like a maturing adolescent, rebellious, anxious to stand on his own feet, and no longer seeking parental support.[53]

The initiator of this present reformation, Bonhoeffer, possessed a balance in his theological position that is not found in many of his extremist followers. Bonhoeffer entertained the possibility and hope of a new form of Christianity, but one that would be radically different from institutionalized religion as it had been known. Particularly did he entertain the hope that there might be a new way to present Christianity which was not based upon what he understood to be the characteristics of traditionally religious man. That is, a weak view of man who could be frightened or forced into asking the particular questions to which religion traditionally had the appropriate answers. Bonhoeffer, like Reinhold Niebuhr, saw evangelism as trying to give people answers to questions which they are not really asking. Bonhoeffer asked whether it was possible to take modern nonreligious, secular man, technologically successful man, and express the meaning of the gospel for him. This is the kind of man who, to use Bishop J. A. T. Robinson's phrase, does not carry around with him a "God-shaped blank" to be filled in through regular church attendance. Thus Bonhoeffer speculated that the future of Christian faith depended upon the possibility of a new formulation, one not based upon man's fears, weaknesses, anxieties, but upon man's strengths, man's sense of his freedom, and man's hope for the future. He raised the issue as to whether Christianity must not begin with an affirmation of man as a responsible person who must not be chided so much as challenged to use his resources to be creative in his life and world.

Thus Bonhoeffer wrote: "Our coming of age forces us to a true recognition of our situation *vis à vis* God. God is teaching us that we must live as men who can get along very well without him. The God who is with us is the God who forsakes us (Mark 15:34). The God who makes us live in this world without using him as a working hypothesis is the God before whom we are ever standing. Before God and with him we live without God. God allows himself to be edged out of the world and on to the cross. God is weak and powerless in the world, and that is exactly the way, the only way, in which he can be with us and help us![54] Contemporary theologians have argued strenuously over the meaning of these words. But what Bonhoeffer appears to be saying is that much of Christianity has promoted the belief in a God that forces immaturity upon his believers. Thus religious faith has produced a kind of human irresponsibility since all the final answers are supposed to be in God's hands. Bonhoeffer read the Biblical witness otherwise. He saw particularly in the life and death of Jesus a belief in a God who refuses to operate in a magical manner. He saw a God who calls men to be responsible for one another, to solve their own problems by drawing upon the resources they have and not turning to religion to provide magical interference for them. This God forces his people to grow into maturity through facing their problems on their own but in his fellowship, i.e., presence.

It is possible to extrapolate out of even this cursory explanation of these three reformations at least four factors which appear to be demonstrated by all of them and which may provide us with some "constants" that characterize all similar kinds of change. The first is that the fundamental issues raised in all of these reformations are never completely solved. The gospel versus law issue, the faith versus works debate, and the secular versus mystical orientations are never settled once and for all. They continue to be current problems. It does not even appear to be possible to answer one of them definitively and then move on to answer another. There is something about these issues that is either endemic to Christianity or even to human nature. The second point is that the dialectical nature of the answers given to these reformation questions appears to produce what must be regarded as a constant dynamic in the institutional expressions of these issues. That is, it is impossible to settle for just one form or expression of the gospel-law dialectic or a faith-works dialectic or a secular-mystical dialectic.

The third point is that all of these reformations involve attempts to restate in the theological expressions and particular circumstances of their times the underlying paradox between freedom and necessity—what might be as over against what must be. Paul Tillich has expressed what he regards to be the essence of the gospel very succinctly in his affirmation that "God accepts the unacceptable in their unecceptableness." This is "good news" because it is a proclamation of freedom. From this good news, he claims, there flow two tremendous liberating powers which transform the life of the individual and produce a unique style which Bonhoeffer further elucidated. The implication is that if God has accepted man in his unacceptableness, then a man is free to be able to accept his unacceptable neighbor. The implication is also that one is liberated to accept oneself. If this is appropriated, then the slavery of attempted self-justification may be broken. Thus Tillich sees in the gospel the roots of a new life-style characteristic of the liberated person who is freed from the great burden of self-justification and freed from the necessity of categorizing everyone else. The reformations then may be seen to revolve around the possibility of being freed to move through the world with a kind of openness, to be vulnerable, and to live the kind of risky life that Christians see in the life-style of Jesus of Nazareth. As Tillich, van Buren, and others view it, this style has the quality of being critical of religion. Jesus' major problems were with the religious functionaries of his day, and he was finally gotten rid of by institutionalized religion of his day because his life was a threat to the religious establishment. Jesus' concern for people expressed itself in part at least in the way in which he tried to liberate them from the institutions that enslaved them.

There may also be some interesting psychological roots and ramifications of the various reformations that have been explored. One of the reasons why they appear to be constant may be, as we have hinted, because they gather up something which is fundamental in the life development of the person. It might be stated that the primacy of the gospel of acceptance finds expression in our initial experience in childhood. That is, the first experience most men have is one of human love and parental acceptance. One might say that the adult man's quest is constantly for a return to something like the freedom of childhood because we are always looking for the kind of acceptance our parents first gave us. It is interesting, in this sense, to note that the experience of faith in the Bible is one that must be expressed in terms of trust. Jesus constantly refers to those who have faith as becoming like little children. Perhaps achieving an understanding of what is meant by the gospel involves a return to the fundamental type of acceptance that we had when we were young. The coming of the law, then, may be associated with the maturation process of the coming into more complete responsibility. Man is understood, Biblically, as the responding and hence the responsible animal. Ethics and good works are not primary but they flow from being accepted. This means that responsibility, moral judgment, and ethics are not primary, but they are important. The freeing experience of acceptance is primary and it is this which makes possible the attitude that asks what the implications are in terms of action in the world. Bonhoeffer and the "death of God" theologians remind us that we must reject a God who acts as a cosmic parent, the one who is perpetually going to look after us so that we can afford to remain infantile. The God who has died, they all agree, is the need fulfiller and problem solver. This kind of God is really dead because he never existed. The meaning of the God seen in Jesus Christ, the God found in the barn in Bethlehem and on the cross at Calvary, is that the living God is of a different nature from the one that provides magic solutions to human problems. This perhaps is the most difficult challenge presented by Christian faith—the challenge to learn to believe in the God Jesus believed in, one who permitted him to go to the cross.

This analysis of the changing reformations within Western religion may assist us to understand something of the way in which religious institutions are being shaken and remolded. But more importantly for the focus of this work, it may help to grasp some aspects of the contemporary revolution and needed reformation in higher education. For, to follow Tillich's argument, the institutional forms of religion within the culture are not limited to those that are specifically ecclesiastical. This would mean that analogous reformatory themes today may be going on in what are regarded as "secular" institutions involving medicine, law, and education. Such issues as a guarantee of annual wage, expanded medical care, racial justice, all may be seen as expressing similar themes to the three reformations we have briefly described.

But the focus of particular attention is more the impact of these insights upon the liberal arts college. The search for identity which characterizes the present student generation and which, as a subject of study, has a long history within higher education may be seen as a reflection of the fundamental question expressed in all three reformations, the nature of the *humanum*—what it is to be a human being. It has been noted that we are rapidly moving into what is called a credential society in which one's acceptance depends upon the ability to master certain techniques. In this issue alone there is to be found an expression of the tension between law and gospel, faith and work, and a secular orientation that seemingly deprives the person of a transcendent value. In the many-faceted rebellions of our youth we find an expression of the desire to be accepted for what one is rather than for what one can do. The instrumentalist ethos of a technological era is perceived by activist students as a threat to fundamental freedom and therefore to humanity. Also prevalent in the actions and words of the student political activist is a cry that men finally learn what it means to be responsible for one another. This includes responsibility for what occurs in Mississippi and in Southeast Asia and Czechoslovakia and Africa. But, most frequently, these issues are not very clearly expressed by students nor understood by the adult generation. One dimension of this problem may be traced back to the difficulty that many young people are finding in overcoming the pervasive mood of adult satisfaction with things as they are and a despair that apparently drives many into a romantic longing for a past that never existed. There is a monolithic inertia in the modern mood—and yet it is set against the tides of inevitable change.

This brief exploration of the history of institutional reform and tentative projection of the possibility of its recurrence should not be concluded without facing the question that the title of this chapter raises. For we are suggesting the possibility of what might be termed a "second magisterial reformation," this time in the college rather than in the church. It must be admitted, however, with some few distinguished exceptions, that there has been very little concerted faculty involvement in this turbulent era of campus activism. When faculty support for change in higher education has been forthcoming, it has generally taken the form of personal professional advisement with only occasional collateral or joint action with student groups. Individual members of faculties have lent support to specific student objectives, but coordinate activity by faculty senates has been weak or nonexistent.

There are many reasons why most faculty seem to lack the reformist zeal of the activist students. In the first place faculty today, as we have noted, identify more with their own professional organizations than they do with a particular college or university. What is more, in a time of an acute shortage of trained personnel in many fields, faculty are highly mobile in the two senses of moving frequently among institutions and being on the go in the course of their sundry consulting activities. Secondly, because of these very opportunities for consultation in government and industry, faculty in some American institutions of higher learning are changing their roles from the traditional classroom- and library-bound model more and more in the direction of the Latin-American model where the faculty have a secondary, though important, allegiance to their colleges but see their primary function in their private activities. Most faculty within the larger universities divide their time between the classroom, research, and professional activity, the latter two frequently in allied institutions within the community. Also, most large colleges and universities are situated in metropolitan centers where virtually all the faculty, if not most of the students, are commuters. Under such circumstances one can scarcely expect the degree of concern over purely college matters that one might expect of a person whose whole life was centered on his campus life and commitments.

Attention has also been directed today to what is termed "the leisure of the theory classes." Scarcity in the academic marketplace and lucrative consultation opportunities have transformed the economic status of many faculty. Most of them are now a part of the affluent segment of society and, as such, many of them reflect the conservative attitude of those who are pretty well satisfied with the *status quo*. Thus many faculty cannot understand why students should get involved in issues of civil rights, poverty, or war when all they have to do is obtain the union card of their diplomas and join the leisured theory class. Each one of these factors that we have noted adds something to the psychological predisposition on the part of many faculty to intellectualize problems rather than to become directly involved in them.

Thus it is difficult to project any large measure of faculty participation in radical educational renewal. John Dewey is said to have observed that while saints are engaged in their contemplation, burly sinners run the world. One might say that while faculty are engaged in their cogitation, the administration and the students tussle over who runs the university.

Does this mean, then, that a second magisterial reformation is impossible or at the least exceedingly unlikely? This may be the case. But if something of the history of the term "magister" is understood, a second revolt of the magisters may be seen as not only a possibility but a present reality. Originally, the master of arts was not an earned academic degree awarded for postbaccalaureate study within the walls of a college or university. The master's degree was given by what was known as "accumulation," that is the accumulation of experience. It was automatically granted to a student after a stipulated period of time of work outside the university after his earning a B.A. degree. Such is still the case at Oxford and Cambridge where, seven terms after graduation, the M.A. is awarded with the payment of an additional small fee. Thus the college graduate was regarded as having become a magister, master, only after practical experience in the world, not just for continued formal study. The ancient universities, of course, were reflecting the prevailing guild system in which the journeyman became a master of his trade only through practical experience in the profession. In this way the early colleges institutionalized the idea that detached study should be balanced, tested, and confirmed by concrete experience. The magister was a person who had both kinds of experience. Thus we recall that the sixteenth-century magisterial reformation was led by men who were academicians, but whose adult experience was not confined to campuses. Luther and Calvin both had extensive experience in the world, in the one case as a parish priest, in the other as a lawyer, before launching upon their careers of reform.

If one applies this criterion of involvement in the world as that which constitutes a magister, then, we may say, that a second magisterial reformation, this time in the colleges, may even now be taking place. In identifying the four overlapping student subcultures, Martin Trow has noted that the protest or activist subculture, numerically the smallest, is the one that is oriented toward the world outside the campus. The activist subculture is caught up in the great social issues of the time and it takes its cues, not so much from what goes on in the university as from what is going on in the world. This group, it might be argued, constitutes something of a modern analogue to the old magisters. Then, too, we would have to observe that there are some faculty members and administrators who are also concerned about and involved in these same social issues. The class of those who comprise the modern magisters may then be larger than one might think—certainly it is influential out of all proportion to its size.

Along this vein it is interesting to project that a new student-faculty grouping may be coming into existence that will be most effective in bringing about constructive change in schools of higher learning. This group may comprise graduate students in some of the key professions such as law, medicine, and architecture. These students, together with "young Turk" faculty members, transcend the negativism of protest.[55] As it has been observed, the rebel is not really free from that which he rebels against. He is tied to that against which he is protesting. This factor, combined with the anti-institutionalism of many of the rebellious activist students, leads them to be almost totally ineffectual in bringing about significant change. But young graduate students are generally not so anti-institutional, although they are frequently perceptively critical of the professional groups within their own disciplines. They recognize that institutions must be scrutinized, judged, and reformed so that they may continue to be channels rather than barriers to those great purposes for which they were originated. Indeed, in our time, all major institutions are being subjected to radical scrutiny as to whether they are helps or hindrances. The most effective criticism naturally comes from those who are also committing themselves to serve as well as criticize these institutions.

Thus, we may be able to say that there are magisters in the colleges and universities today, students and faculty who not only have or are acquiring the detached, expert knowledge, but who are also involved in placing that knowledge at the service of meeting the pressing social needs of the world. These magisters may assist in the bringing about of a second magisterial reformation that will transform the colleges and universities of our country as radically as did their earlier counterparts reform the church.

7

Establishing an Ethos for Change: Mood, Motivation, and Militancy

WE HAVE STRESSED that the contemporary knowledge explosion, for which colleges and universities are so largely responsible, has produced the modern technological era. Technology, in turn, has been responsible for the limited kinds of revolutionary activity which we have seen characterize our world. But it may be asserted that this same technology also provides new ingredients for extending creative change to other areas of life thereby bringing about solutions to a number of what seem so far to be insoluble problems. Many of these troublesome problems arise just because the fruits of the knowledge explosion have not been fully applied nor extended to specific areas or groups in society. The problem of poverty is an obvious example.

One of the chief dilemmas faced today centers not on how to acquire new knowledge but on how to apply reasonably what is already known to issues such as poverty, race, war, and the population explosion. It is imperative that those factors which inhibit or even prohibit the application of the knowledge in hand and the techniques already available be identified. When one sets about to make this identification one soon runs into the problem of dealing with the total ethos of society, i.e., what goes into making up the prevailing cultural mood. This ethos is a very complex admixture of historical accidents, cultural heritages, attitudinal stances, national and personal self-images, class fears, and individual superstitions. These are some of the factors that constitute the *Zeitgeist* of culture.

Commentators on the contemporary cultural scene have frequently characterized the modern mood of Western culture as that of hesitancy, despair, emptiness—a feeling of being trapped. This is far more than the relatively simple matter of Western societies having come to the end of their geographic frontiers. Close to the beginning of this century, Paul Tillich identified the modern *Zeitgeist* as stemming from a malaise he termed "spiritual anxiety." This, he said, was occasioned by the sense of loss of meaning within Western cultures. In its relative form this anxiety expresses itself in a sense of emptiness, while in its absolute form it paralyzes with the threat of total meaninglessness. Thus it frequently happens that those who have achieved what is regarded as success, defined in terms of the contemporary culture, also find that despite this achievement, life appears empty and they are haunted with the specter of a totally meaningless existence.

Now it must be remembered that intellectual systems and cultural forms do not cease to hold the allegiance of their devotees or prove unconvincing because some fatal flaw is belatedly discovered within them. Rather, it would appear they fail because of a shift in what we are calling the cultural mood. What was convincing at one period within history is not in another.[56] For example, up until quite recently the way one established the truth of an idea or the validity of a document was by ascribing it to a much earlier age. This reflected the belief in the existence of a golden age in the past, the closer to which one could get, the more veracity one could claim. This accounts for the ascription of earlier dates and authors to many ancient documents which were forced to claim antiquity for their ideas in order to be accepted. Today, in our modern era, just the opposite appears to be the case. The latest ideas, inventions, and products are regarded as having the greatest claim upon us just because of their newness.

Because it is somewhat amorphous, the whole matter of cultural mood is difficult although not impossible to assess. Artists, poets, playwrights, philosophers, and theologians are, to varying degrees, sensitive in portraying and analyzing elements of this ethos. Many diverse factors may be seen as helping to constitute the cultural mood and shifts in it. Identifying these factors has been the subject of some of the great intellectual analyses of the modern era. Because of the attraction of monistic systems, the tendency has been to identify a single factor as the determinative one influencing all developments. In the nineteenth century the concept of social evolution was derived from biological evolution and applied to societies with the result that in the West the pervasive cultural ethos justified colonization and exploitation as inevitable expressions of competition for the survival of the fittest. The life cycle of birth, maturation, and decline was applied by analysts to human societies and their spirit of optimism or pessimism was seen to be reflective of which stage they were thought to be in. German idealist philosophers, for example Hegel and Schopenhauer, identified such amorphous agents as "the World Spirit" as being responsible for the directions in which history was moving. Marx was among the first to assert the function of the economy as the determinative factor. Today Marshall McLuhan has selected the technology supporting the media as the factor bringing about fundamental change in our society. Abram Kardiner, Kurt Lewin, Margaret Mead, and Norman O. Brown have applied a variety of psychological insights to the problem of unpacking the dominant features of a society. One of the differences between the outlook of the student generation making up the new left and the older Marxists is the students' acceptance of psychological factors as being of equal importance with economics in accounting for the behavior of nations. It is this blending of Freud and Marx that has enabled these students to maintain a critical posture vis-à-vis both American and Russian foreign policy.[57] It could be argued that a liberal arts curriculum which included an exploration of the contributions of figures such as Tillich, McLuhan, Marcuse, Jourard, and Brown would be well on its way in providing students with insights into the present *Zeitgeist* as well as the critical tools for dealing with it creatively.

In such a curriculum the study of philosophy would include, in addition to the traditional introductory and survey courses, extensive study in existentialism and linguistic analysis. But particular attention would be focused on those philosophers who have contributed to the development of social theory. Thus the role of reason would be examined not only as it functions as detached critic but as the primary tool for promoting cultural change. The psychology curriculum would not only involve an introduction to experimental psychology, but the behavioristic tradition would be balanced by reading in the "new" humanistic psychology. It would also be possible to devise an educational philosophy to support such a curriculum that was aware and made use of the new technology which is influencing the field of mass communication. Thus the curriculum could take into account the necessity of restoring McLuhan's haptic balance. Such a curriculum would demonstrate the way in which the content of any technology is, as McLuhan emphasizes, always that of the previous technological era so that enlightened social criticism is a perpetual necessity. A reordered curriculum could also be set within a type of Tillichian philosophical framework which attests to the profound importance of culture as the embodiment of man's ultimate concerns. Tillich's understanding of the way in which finite forms and their contents may be transparent to the Ground of Being held in tension with his critical Protestant Principle, which rejects any identification of these forms with the ultimate, would provide a conceptual framework within which it would be possible to cope with the apparent lack of any pervasive meaning in our society.

Success in any such restructuring of liberal arts education, providing an ethos for a rational appreciation of change, should also contribute to overcoming the inertia that surrounds the traditional departmental structures with their vested academic interests. It would also be dedicated to reducing the internecine warfare that goes on in "monochrome" departments through focusing their attention on an issue-oriented curriculum. This curriculum would test the contribution of a school of thought both by the way in which it illuminated the issues and by the way it contributed positively to the solution of the great social problems.

But attempting to arrange for continuing representation of many varied commitments within the major disciplines is not the only kind of concern that a liberal arts administrator must have. There is, in addition, the problem of maintaining a balance between the rightful claims of the individual faculty member and student and the claims of the academic community and the broader political community as well. Paul Tillich has noted that solutions to the fundamental question of the courage to be involve a rightful adjudication between the courage to be as an individual and the courage to be as a part of the larger community. He has also noted that where the emphasis is upon personal rights there develops a value orientation determined by the concept of the fulfillment of individual potentialities. Where the person is stressed at the expense of the demands of the community then whatever contributes to the enrichment of personal experience is what is valued. But where the emphasis is upon the claims of the community what appears to be convincing is defined in terms of that which serves perceived collective needs. The great problem is, of course, finding some suitable balance between the claims of these two forms of existence. Some form of compromise between them actually has always been the fact. No totally individual experience is possible and no collective experience, no matter how confining, has totally disregarded the needs of all the individuals comprising it. Unfortunately, in a majority of cases, balance is not achieved and the result is either an individualism which isolates and finally contributes to the feeling of emptiness and meaninglessness or a collectivist society which stifles personal expression and snuffs out individual creativity.

Much more attention must be given to the primary institutions of our society, each of which has to deal with the claims of the individual and of the group and the balance that institution achieves or fails to achieve contributes to the ethos and mood of the culture. There may be, on the part of many, a temptation to acquiesce today to a kind of fatalism as if the prevailing mood or ethos were totally beyond human comprehension or intelligent control. It is true that in all eras of social upheaval there is an increase in attitudes reflecting despair, as illustrated by a rise in interest in astrology, superstition, etc. This is because, for some, it appears to be preferable that an identifiable even if irrational power be in control of the affairs of men and of nations than it be a matter of blind chance and/or free choice.

If the colleges and universities are the key institutions dedicated to the extension of rational control over environment and to the reasonable solution of man's most pressing problems, then these institutions must make it clear by the way in which they operate that they see reason playing a determinative function in the world. The college must demonstrate to a student generation, increasingly unsympathetic with an intellectual detachment that seems to serve things as they are, that detachment may also produce social criticism that changes society by dealing creatively with its primary problems.

A good part of the outcome to this weighty issue revolves around the question of trust. For it is a question whether those who are making the decisions have what is ultimately a faith conviction that the result of the combined intellectual resources of the various disciplines may make for radical but rational change. There are many who feel that almost any alteration of things as they are at present will bring about situations of anarchy and nihilism. But the socially concerned and politically active members of this student generation are in many ways expressing trust that brand-new structures and not chaos may result from radical change.

Perhaps it could be argued that it was easier to manifest this kind of trust in the past when the patterns involved were not themselves the product of human creation but an order which was regarded to be objectively "out there" in nature. But, in fact, even the scientists are now aware that the so-called laws of nature are not in the natural order but are the products of the human intervention that observation entails. Thus trust in the patterns and forms of nature must now be seen as involving trust in human reason. Rather than precluding change, this should encourage the taking of risks in order to achieve a greater rationality. The whole process of evolution having brought itself to depend upon the outcome of human choice, as Teilhard de Chardin observed, we can afford to take rationally determined risks. While it is true that it is extremely difficult to tell whether changes brought about by human decision are going to be totally beneficial or harmful (as we have seen in the advent of the ecological crisis), the solution to this problem certainly does not lie in any attempt to go backward. The answer is not less rational control, but more. The application of computers to the great social dilemmas brings about the possibility of a whole new range of model testing. Before one is committed to a certain choice one may determine many of the results of this course of action through the use of the computer. This approach must be vastly expanded and applied throughout all higher education.

It has been said that ours is an era characterized by a failure of nerve on the part of those who are making the key decisions in every area of life. This mood makes for a repetition of what were regarded as the right or safe decisions in the past. But what is required are new imaginative approaches to the besetting problems of our time. Aside from our political institutions, no other structure is in more need of such imagination than the college or university. But again it must be reiterated that behind this willingness to risk lies the crisis in the area of trust. This trust, as we have noted, bears a close resemblance to the category traditionally known as religious faith. A contemporary "secular" expression of this faith is the conviction that the constellation of values and the structures of the present society have not achieved perfection and that most of them need radical transformation. This radical judgment is set in the context of an equally firm conviction; first, that the integrative process is still at work and that, when critically analyzed and changed, new patterns more rational and just may be discovered or developed. It also implies the belief that the new patterns need not simply be those impressed upon the objective world by the subjective willfulness of those in power but may be a synergistic expression of a subject-object unity which is man's unique function in reality.

There are resources in liberal arts colleges which would justify striking out in new directions to establish these new goals and to demonstrate that cultivation of reason for purposes of social criticism and change. Perhaps one of the simplest differences between a theistic and an atheistic secularity may be seen in the fact that the former regards pattern and meaning as something that man discovers, reshapes, and helps to create, while the latter regards them as only subjectively real, imposed by man upon what is essentially a meaningless universe. Thus it may be argued that the creation of an ethos or mood that invites critical participation and radical recreation is fundamentally a matter of religious conviction. The faithful faculty member and administrator in a secular age may not be the one who holds or does not hold certain propositions about God, Jesus, or the afterlife. He may rather be the one who dares to affirm and live by the affirmation that meanings are there in the universe to be discovered by man who also assists in their articulation. This kind of faith necessarily involves the ability to live through, to accept, and to encourage change.

Now it must be admitted that change has always seemed to pose a threat to man. Perhaps it may be traced back to the fear of being lost, being deprived of one's familiar orientation which must have been most alarming to primitive man as it still is to little children. If the environment changes, then we feel lost. The fear of change may also reflect something that is fundamental to man's thinking process. Man uses concepts and concepts are static, frozen. When something for which I have had a concept changes, then my mental furniture seems to be disarranged. For whatever reasons, from the beginning, change appears to have been a threat and a constant source of anxiety. Indeed, for long periods of human history and even in some places today, human life is short and full of travail. There appears to be no time for thoughtful change; just clinging to life is problematic enough. Thus, in the long painful struggle for civilization, change has seemed a threat to the few hard-won gains; it still seems a threat to those whose battle cry is "law and order" today.

Very early in man's development, therefore, he looked for that which was changeless, permanent. The ideal became security from change and this search for permanence became a prominent and permanent part of man's religion. To the Greek mind, that which changed was inferior to what was conceived to be changeless. The unchanging concepts or ideas became more valued than the changing, growing reality which they originally reflected. Thus Greek philosophy became engaged in the search for what was really real and this was identical with what did not change.

From Greek philosophy this conception entered into Christian theology. The quite unbiblical idea that God was unchangeable became an important part of Christian intellectual baggage. Its popular expression may be found in the hymn "Abide with Me" with its lines "Change and decay in all around I see. O Thou, who changest not, abide with me."

But an exploration of the Scriptures reveals that the idea of the changeless or eternal quality of God is balanced by the conception of God as the Lord of change. There appears to be a fundamental division between two types of religion. There are those which celebrate the repetitiveness of nature and its changelessness. These nature religions are security-oriented. There are in contrast the historical religions. In them God is revealed within the changes that characterize man's historical experiences. Although rooted in primitive nature religions, Judaism and Christianity are historically oriented. One may see this in the Passover cele-brations in Judaism in which the egg and spring plants show the nature origin of the festival which was overlayed with the historical experience of the exodus out of Egypt. The mythical rites of reviving spring are still displayed in the Easter eggs and bunny rabbits. Judaism and Christi-anity have found God active in the changing events of political history recorded in Scripture: in the exodus, the Babylonic captivity, the life of the historical Jesus. In the Bible there is the conviction that, as J. A. T. Robinson has noted with respect to morality, God is to be found in the rapids as well as in the rocks. He is to be found in change, in the flux of history as well as in those values which abide.

What distinguishes the position we are trying to eluci-date from the desire for change just for the sake of change or novelty, what separates it from the fretful reordering of the utopian who rejects anything but a perfect "system," is the recognition that in achieving change there is cost and loss. Unless there is the recognition not only of the social and individual cost of change, but of the fact that in change something of unique value is also sacrificed, always hope-fully for something of greater value, it would be impossible to claim for any period of history any meaning in itself save insofar as it anticipated or contributed to a final perfected stage. It must be affirmed that each stage of history incor-porates unique values which make it meaningful to those who live in it, so that there is significance in the various parts of the process as well as in any final fulfillment of it.

In a sense what is being pleaded for is a kind of militancy on the part of students, administrators, and faculty. This term used so widely today produces many negative reactions. But the term has the virtue of underscoring the active, critical role that institutions of higher learning must begin to play in society. For too long a time they have been the uncritical servants to a host of needs of this society. They must become more vocal and active critics. The term "militancy" may describe a type of social criticism which also involves action. The term also has other advantages since it not only carries with it connotations of change and action but also implies the recognition of opposition; there are powerful entrenched forces within the educational establishment opposed to change. Furthermore, it reminds us of the need for strategic planning, discipline, and sacrifice, all actions which have been traditionally associated with the military. It must be admitted that the term also has negative implications because of its relatively recent use by members of the Black Power civil rights movements. These negative connotations include willfulness, the arbitrary use of power, and subversion. But similar to the conception of Black Power itself, when it is properly understood, the term "militancy" is not without value. For centuries Christians referred to their earthly institutional expression as the "Church Militant." This idea carried with it the conception of a need for change as the church considered itself fighting the forces of evil which held the world captive. In our time there is desperate need for the College Militant dedicated to the application of critical reason to changing society in a world that will either change creatively or die violently. The function that the eschatological hope of the church has performed is to hold out both the possibility and the inevitability of a radically new order which will involve drastic change. Faith in this coming rule of God is what enabled men and women in the past to resist the false claims of the

established order. Norman O. Brown sees in the eschatological hope of the resurrection of the body a witness to the
possibility of a very different order of human life, one which
overcomes man's alienation from himself—his separation
from and rejection of his body. He argues that, to the extent
that they have held before men the possibility of a radically
different order, the "naïve" religious conservatives are
preferable to the liberals who have only too easily preached
accommodation to the prevailing order, advocating only
the possibility of ameliorative action. The kind of trust in
the cognitive process that will yield order when rational
criticism is directed to social change, could be regarded as
the modern "secular" equivalent to traditional eschatology.
Young people, by their sacrifice and seeming recklessness,
may be exhibiting this kind of faith. It is time that professional educators indicated a willingness to match it with a
similar kind of risky affirmation and action.

Obviously what is involved is a very thorough reordering
of the entire life of the college and the university. But this
reordering will also contain elements of continuity with the
past roles that institutions of higher learning have played in
Western society. The proposals that are made, therefore,
have an element of continuity as well as discontinuity about
them. They are, because of their scope and the cost involved, immodest. But compared with the possibilities they
may offer and the inevitable consequences of less radical
restructuring of college life—they may prove most modest
indeed.

8

An Immodest Proposal: Toward Reforming Liberal Arts Education

IT HAS BEEN our contention that what is needed is a thoroughgoing analysis of the directions in which liberal arts education should proceed for the remainder of this century and into the twenty-first. Intelligent changes can be made if those responsible for making them have vision and daring. But changes will occur whether or not they are made rationally, i.e., through a process involving dialogue and mutuality of interest. If this is not the case, decisions will then be the product of frustrated protest and emotional reaction rather than the application of critical reason in a dialectical process devoted to the discovery of new forms of educational achievements for all segments of society.

It has been argued that the renewal of higher education must, among other things, involve renewal within the humane disciplines. But this renewal of the humanities is not simply a matter of curricular reform, however constant, of tinkering with the departmental structures or of revising course requirements. The transformation of the humanities requires asking fundamental questions about what kinds of experience students need to meet the challenges of life in the twenty-first century. This, in turn, involves a radical reappraisal of what is known as General Education, this term referring to those courses which are regarded as providing the common core that ought to be the heritage of all liberally educated men and women.

But when one goes into anything deeply one soon finds oneself involved rather broadly. Thus we might suspect that the upgrading of the humanities or the reform of General Education may well lead to the consideration of the creation of a new kind of humanism. Just as Renaissance humanism grew out of a synthesis of classical and Christian elements, so a new humanism will undoubtedly involve a blending of the older humanism with elements of the new scientific technology. This new humanism in its this-worldly, immanentist orientation and its sensate eudaemonism may well have much in common with elements of modern, radical theological thought.

Indeed, it is possible to claim that the reform of liberal arts education is, from a Tillichian theological perspective, fundamentally a religious matter. Religion here is, of course, being conceived of in Tillich's sense as having to do with man's ultimate concerns. Again, it is our contention that, in this secular era, the college in some ways more than the church performs or is called upon to perform such basic religious tasks as answering for an increasing majority of the better educated questions regarding the nature and destiny of man and of what constitutes highest value and meaning. If the college can capitalize upon its newly found freedom from direct ecclesiastical control and avoid falling under political control or other forms of captivity, its independent stance should provide a setting for the application of critical reason to the pressing problems of society. Because the college has been by heritage a "universal" institution, it may perform this task without the limitations that the particularism of past faith commitments have imposed upon the churches. Thus for the first time the colleges and universities may really begin to express their long-claimed ideal of embracing the universal company of scholars.

In the light of this situation a proposal might be put forward that would challenge the churches to recognize the radical reformation transpiring in modern secular society and also that would provide them with an opportunity to demonstrate that institutional as well as personal lives are found by risking them or even losing them for the sake of the gospel. This proposal could take its clue from what happened in the 1920's when the Church of England was disestablished in Wales. When this was done, part of the relatively large ecclesiastical endowments that supported the established church were used to establish the University of Wales. The argument which underlay this action was that the endowment was a contribution by Welshmen down the ages to the functioning of what was regarded to be an institution of consummate value to society. In the twentieth century, when many Welshmen had forsaken the established church and the culture had other pressing needs, the endowment, it was felt, could appropriately be used to support higher education.

Most Protestant denominations—and indeed all American religious groups—have superfluous or marginal churches and/or properties that are not used to their fullest advantage. Many small-town and rural congregations cannot support full-time pastors. Churches also own city real estate that no longer is creatively related to the needs of their dwindling urban membership. The new era of ecumenical cooperation has also made possible the consolidation of church facilities and overlapping boards and agencies that could more efficiently and economically serve the needs of their congregations, denominations, and communities.

It would be possible for these religious bodies to pool their resources, disposing of or leasing superfluous properties, and to use the funds achieved to provide better support for their own more academically sound church-related colleges. They could also help the campus ministries that are currently threatened by the shortage of funds and are searching for new sources of support. These funds could also support or partially endow departments of religion in the larger colleges and universities across the country. The contribution of these kinds of support would provide an opportunity for important conversations between the religious groups and institutions of higher learning. Such conversations have, of course, been taking place and church bodies have made some enlightened pronouncements in recent years regarding higher education. But the colleges have been slow to hear because the religious groups, unlike government, industry, or the large foundations, had nothing to offer but good advice. The proposal put forward here would guarantee a serious consideration by institutions of higher learning of the many important insights that religion might bring to bear on American education. These conversations would make possible, for example, a thorough exploration of the whole learning process, perhaps along lines that we have indicated.

It is also important to remember that the churches have a much longer history of direct service in attempting to meet the kinds of urban problems now being faced for the first time by the universities. Thus the churches could contribute much to institutions of higher education as they explore this new role for themselves. What has been called the campus ministry is now increasingly being seen as having a wider responsibility—relating to urban ministries —that can provide a channel for relating the colleges to urban services.

It could also be argued that a portion of the funds that the religious groups might provide to the colleges ought to go into the humanities in general and not just to support teaching in the field of religion. In an era of massive government and industry grants to the sciences, support for the humanities is desperately needed. It is altogether fitting that religious groups stress the stake that they have in the forming of human beings—the essential task of all the humane disciplines. Some formula for dividing support among these areas of concern could be worked out. For example, a third of the money might be given to support the humanities, a third go to the campus ministries, and a third toward providing for formal instruction in religion. It would, of course, be imperative that there be no attempt to reassert sectarian control by the churches over the colleges or universities because of these contributions. Both commitment to the ideal of the unfettered pursuit of truth and the experience that a secular, religiously neutral environment is actually the best setting for a vigorous religious life should confirm the churches in their resolve not to attempt to exert direct control over even their own colleges, let alone independent or state institutions.

Local churches and synagogues could further assist the educational task by providing loci for exposure to and service in society. College personnel could use such settings for a variety of extension services. Young people in these locales could be provided with the transforming experience that has generally been reserved for faculty—that of learning a subject by having to teach it to someone else. Every new teacher knows this to be true by experience, but we have restricted this opportunity to a very few students.

Although it should not count upon it, the church in bequeathing an endowment of money, personnel, and experience to colleges would be acting in a manner that might secure its own future institutional viability. As we will note, the indigenous religion of the modern college campus is in need of the long experience represented in the Judeo-Christian heritage. Support given to the colleges in terms of departments of religion and a strengthened campus ministry would ensure the contribution of the best of these heritages to the total educational milieu. It might further be suggested in this connection that, as has already been discussed in the Association of American Theological Schools, seminary education should be related to a university. The church should not continue to educate its professionals in isolation from the mainstream of academic life. Theological education should be presumed to have important contributions to offer other disciplines and professions.

But if the college, because of the default of institutional religion and a shift in the cultural mood, is to perform a quasi-ecclesiastical function, it cannot rest content with its traditional, isolated, ivory-tower role with respect to society. The college must use its primary product—the critical reason—for the reform or salvation of society. The argument commonly heard against a social-action role for institutions of higher learning is that direct involvement jeopardizes the needed objectivity which educational institutions ought to have and which is their most important contribution to society. But this argument ignores several important factors. It fails to take into account the mood of the present student generation which, as we have seen, is in the process of rejecting a conception of reason that does not appear to modify things as they are or enrich immediate experience. And it also negates the fact that objective, critical analysis is but the first step in the application of reason to the solution of human problems and that institutions of higher learning cannot limit themselves to part of the total learning process.

What really lies behind the rejection of a partisan or advocacy role for colleges and universities is the fear that direct involvement will bring about reprisals, primarily economic, against them. But it should be recognized that since change is bound to occur, the application of reflective reason to this change in institutions with their roots deep in Western culture is the safest way of dealing with change and may ultimately be less damaging to the present order. It is when the forces making for change meet irrational, implacable, and intransigent opposition that the resulting clash is so broadly destructive.

Proponents of the objective or detached view of higher education often fail to point out that the position they espouse does not really make for a nonpartisan role on the part of colleges or universities. What actually occurs is that detached higher education serves the present order of things by supplying the goods and services which those who support it feel are needed. The rash of student protests against some types of government and industrial recruiting on campuses indicates how aware many students are of the actual commitments of "neutral" colleges.

The university that shuns an advocacy role with respect to involvement in its indigenous community and chooses just to train experts who may or may not use their expertise to solve community problems is actually acting in a political fashion. It is abdicating responsibility to those who happen to wield power in society. Colleges and universities do not really have the option to choose to be nonpolitical, or non-controversial. They may only choose the nature and form of their inevitable involvement and implicit commitments.

Certainly an application of the advocacy role would eventuate in a far more volatile educational scene. Debate, challenge, experiment, and counterexperiment would characterize college and university life. But, after all, these phenomena are but indications of great dynamism. American higher education is much more vital today just because of the activist students, the protest movements, the sit-ins, the demonstrations, than it was in the placid days of the uncommitted, waiting, silent, beat generation. One of the characteristics of the contemporary student is his tolerance of conflictual elements and recognition that they are part and parcel of life. Educators, too, must be prepared to accept and even welcome conflict within higher education.

If the Tillichian thesis is taken seriously, that religion is expressed in every structure and institution of culture, then the college may be seen as incorporating a basically re-ligious function. Just as in Tillich's writings where his con-cept of the "latent" church is much more exciting than was his understanding of the institutional church, so it is that many students and faculty find in institutions of higher learning a type of community, tolerant of disagreement and creative in conflict, that is more relevant to their world than what is found in much present-day institutional religion. For despite the penetrating insights of the official theolo-gies, there is little authentic community and almost no tolerance for conflict within the congregational life of American churches.

Thus a formal religious vacuum exists on the contemporary college scene. But it is possible to identify in college life, especially among the activist student groups, substitutes for certain traditional aspects of church life. A kind of gospel of student freedom is being preached that will liberate young men and women from the law so often identified with the *in loco parentis* tradition. Students manifest something akin to the New Testament diaconate, i.e., service to the needy in the outside world expressed in terms of remedial tutorial projects, involvement in civil rights issues and in antiwar and antipoverty movements. Among some students a semireligious life-style is discernible which sometimes infuriates parents with its imprudent, other-worldliness. The widespread craze for new forms of music and the experimentation in drugs constitute involvement in a kind of liturgy and sacrament. Writing on the use of drugs by college students, Jeremy Larner has noted: "The novice is . . . equipped with drugs, priests for parents, and fellow acolytes for siblings. The members of the drug family are connected not by birth and mortality, but by destiny and salvation. They reinforce their new personalities with common rituals and in-group language, and —above all—the taking of the sacraments."[58] The primitive Christian agape gathering may even be secularly reflected in the modern "love-in." But much of this indigenous campus religion is desperately in need of the perspective and content of the great classical religious traditions. Yet these traditions are woefully lacking in most institutions which are without instruction in religion or virtually so.

Much is said and written today about religious institutions having to recognize their transition into a post-Constantinian or even post-Christian era. While this transition is proceeding in society at large at different rates of speed, it has virtually already been completed within colleges and universities. Save for a very few institutions, the withdrawal of direct ecclesiastical control has been completed within Protestantism and is currently beginning to take place in Catholic colleges and universities. State institutions, by and large, never did have religious connections nor did they include religion as a subject matter for research and teaching. How religion as a discipline is faring within the new post-Constantinian context is of more than general interest, for it constitutes part of the needed renewal of the humanities.

Except for a few centers of higher learning where tradition preserved them, religious studies were not a staple in college education throughout most of the country in the twentieth century. But since World War II a dramatic increase in the number of religion departments has taken place with vastly expanded enrollment in their courses. Initially, these course offerings were in the field of what was known as comparative religion and formed part of the attempt to break out of the parochialism of the Western cultural tradition. Gradually, the study of Christianity and Judaism developed alongside the study of the non-Western religions. It has become recognized that the field of religion is better studied in a setting denominationally neutral than in a church-controlled institution which may be regarded as biased. Three primary arguments are being put forward for the reintroduction of religious studies within college curricula. The first is the very nature of the curriculum itself which, if it lived up to its inclusive nature, could scarcely leave out of consideration such a major human preoccupation. The second is recognition of the failure of the church's own Sunday church school program and the need to understand religious traditions if other humane disciplines (particularly in the field of literature) are to be understood. There is also the matter of increased demand on the part of students for courses in this area. Although it surprises many parents and faculty who came out of a more skeptical era, students with few personal religious commitments are nonetheless eager to have oppor-

tunities provided for the study of the major religious traditions. But in addition to these three widely recognized
factors, there are other reasons for the phenomenal recent
increase in interest in the study of religion. One is the re-
linquishing by much of philosophy of its traditional task of
providing an overarching meaning system for education.
Many large philosophy departments have become dominated by linguistic analysis, and students who might normally have had their interest disciplined by philosophical
study, turn to religion departments that are still dealing
with primary issues of meaning and value. Also, as a member of the first totally post-Puritan generation, the college
student of the late twentieth century feels free to explore
religion without fear of being overwhelmed or strait-
jacketed by religious commitment. He is neither predisposed to reject religion because of its claims upon him
nor to accept it because it is part of his cultural heritage.
Religion may be looked at as containing a variety of possible
solutions to aspects of modern man's pressing problems.
There is also the factor of student exposure to a type of
religion that is an actual factor in the growing social crisis.
The role of the Negro churches in the civil rights movement, the principal denominations' support of selective
conscientious objection as well as the involvement of religious leaders in the war on poverty have all awakened
interest on the part of students in what might be called
revolutionary elements within the Judeo-Christian heritage.
There is also the factor that in studying religion a student
becomes aware that he is involved in a discipline in which
theory cannot be separated from practice and in which
experience is of vital importance. Living in an experience-
oriented culture but feeling experientially deprived, many
students find religion a fascinating field of interest.

Although it may not be explicitly recognized, there is
some evidence that the student interest in the academic
study of religion is an indication of a desire for direct kinds
of experience. Especially is this true where the study of

religion takes place under a neutral sponsorship with no danger of the student being forced to commit himself. It may therefore be argued that the support of religious studies is a most important factor in the renewal of liberal arts education. Certainly departments of religion together with the more perceptive chaplaincies and campus ministries have been generally alert to and involved in challenging the neutralist conception of the college's role, in leading demands for educational reform, and in supporting the incorporation of minority groups and cultures into higher education.

If the college is to adopt the somewhat ecclesiastical role, which it is argued as possessing whether it likes it or not, there are certain features of the educational experience that certainly must be taken into account in the sense of intellectual awareness of them, and in the sense of how they impinge upon this new churchly role. Certainly these factors must be in the foreground of attention in any contemplated curricular changes, in upgrading the humanities, and particularly in the reform of General Education. It is impossible, at this point, to deal adequately with the extremely difficult problems posed by the return of General Education. Not being trained, nor claiming professional competence in this field, it is unlikely that we should be able to succeed where so many experts confess to be baffled. Nonetheless, there would appear to be certain aspects of the problem that any proposed reform of General Education should take into account.

In the past few years there has been something of a disenchantment with what are termed General Education programs in colleges and universities. A few of the reasons why the General Education programs are in trouble are obvious: the increased emphasis by departments on their own programs, which has brought about an acceleration of specialization; upgraded programs in secondary schools, which in some instances provide equivalents of the old General Education courses; the impossibility of discovering a consensus as to what it is that every college man and woman should have read, studied, or possessed in common; finally, the sheer structural and logistical complexity of maintaining a General Educational program. George Waggoner has expressed something of this critical attitude in his observation that General Education curricula have "suffered from naïveté, over-simplification and institutionalization."[59] Faculty members often object to General Education programs because they deprive departments from early access to the freshmen. Also, faculty in the field of the sciences generally feel that those who teach in General Education programs are frequently not themselves scientifically oriented. They tend, they argue, to be "idea" rather than "method" or "experimentally" oriented. These faculty therefore complain that students are introduced into the scientific disciplines by those who do not represent the essential nature of those disciplines.

It is true that some secondary schools have in recent years greatly enriched their curricula so as to include a wider range of subject matter in the general field of culture and Western civilization. But this development has been by no means uniform throughout the country so that this background cannot be counted on by colleges or universities in admitting their freshmen. More significantly, it may well be asked whether high school students are at an age to benefit most from this kind of enriched curriculum. Some evidence appears to indicate that students are more receptive to the broadening and leavening influence of General Education when they have arrived at their more mature college years.[60]

It may also be argued that the departments within a college would benefit from retaining some kind of General Education program permitting them to specialize to a far greater extent on the upper-class level than they are at present. Though admittedly deprived of earlier contact with potential majors, the specialized departments might find themselves dealing with better-prepared students possessing a broader and more adequate background as the basis for the specialization that they would then be prepared to undertake with superior preparation.

Undoubtedly the strongest argument for a new approach to General Education is that it would give to the teaching and learning process the emphasis that it deserves. Despite all the theoretical objections that may be mustered, it must be admitted that, given the necessary emphasis upon increasing specialization, the almost exclusively research-oriented teacher cannot find the time to spend in striving for excellence in instruction. There are, however, numbers of extremely well-prepared faculty members in most colleges whose particular genius lies precisely in the area of communication and who, while not eschewing research, find their vocational fulfillment in teaching rather than exclusively in research relationships. One need not confuse good teaching with student popularity nor set up a meaningless dichotomy between research and teaching to be convinced that excellence in teaching can be evaluated both by students and by faculty colleagues. This certainly would be the case in any program of General Education in which team teaching and close faculty-student and instructional relationships were the norms. There are faculty who regard themselves as generalists who at the same time are specialists in a particular field.

In a very real sense, the working out of the details of a General Education curriculum is a relatively minor problem. Indeed, if the prior problems of obtaining interdepartmental cooperation and a competent faculty committed to teaching were solved, then any number of good curricula might be devised.

The focus of such a General Education program should be upon the student, recognizing that early in his academic career he needs the experience of wide-ranging intellectual quests. It has been noted that the feeling, valuing aspects of the student's experiences are largely left untouched by most college life today. Yet a liberal education should be one which aims to deepen and broaden feeling as well as thought. It should also be stressed that the most significant locus for the integration of knowledge is not in the curriculum, however new and exciting, but in the student's mind. Cultural shock, one of the fruits of overseas educational ventures, is widely recognized as a unique benefit to the total educational experience. Hopefully, this kind of shock might be provided for some of the students by overseas programs which have expanded in almost all colleges and universities. But something of the same kind of experience could be provided for by involvement in the community at large—particularly within the city. It is imperative that these programs be available for a larger proportion of students than is generally now the case. A General Education program should have three major purposes. First, it should aim to help the student learn some ways of thinking about important aspects of the world. There should not be any worry about the completeness of this systematic knowledge nor the extensiveness of the specific facts gained; rather, the purpose would be to have students engaged in real depth thinking in selected areas in order to have these ways of thinking become meaningful and usable parts of their mental skills. Then, they should begin to understand the mode of thought characteristic of the physical sciences to appreciate that mode and to some extent be able to use it. The same should be true of the humanities and social sciences.

The second general goal should be to increase the students caring about learning. The need to learn, which is natural for a young man or woman, must be freed of many of the blocks put in the way of learning by earlier educational, social, and personal experiences. It is one of the hallmarks of the liberally educated person that he cares about his own and others' growth in knowledge and understanding. The third goal of the educational program should be some understanding of the learning process itself. Although part of this is attitudinal, as we have just stated, part is also a cognitive skill involving an understanding of how to explore, acquire knowledge, assimilate facts, reason logically, and think intuitively.

It is not possible to structure this kind of learning experience precisely; part of it comes from living in a milieu where knowledge is valued and research practiced. It is the primary role of General Education to provide such a milieu. It is universally agreed that it is desirable to have greater variety within any curriculum and more opportunity for independent research and testing of ideas. Obviously a curriculum must provide for experiences such as an "urban semester" or a "developing nations semester" in which the focus of entire blocks of time could be devoted to the problems of the city or of the developing segment of the world community of nations.

In the modern era that which was merely a theoretical desideratum has become more than a technical possibility—it has become an immediate imperative. The increasing interrelatedness of the problems of the contemporary world, the vastly increased means of communication made available by science and technology, the worldwide responsibility of educated nations, all make for obsolescence of an educational system which could be regarded as parochial because of its exclusive preoccupation with Western culture. In the world of tomorrow what are now referred to as the developing nations will occupy new and important positions—so will minority cultures in our society, black and brown and yellow. Students today must understand something of the coming of age of these dynamic new cultures—a learning that is as important as the knowledge of the rise of the Western world.

In charting the goals and objectives of any college, it is necessary to take into account the resources of that college including the entire community as well as other educational institutions nearby. Colleges could expand their rather modest cooperative programs with government and the private sector by providing opportunities for students to alternate exposure or work semesters with reflective academic semesters. The private sector should be able to contribute VISTA-type support to students in exchange for modest services. Consortia of every kind are helpful ways of meeting the expense of certain types of education. One of the institutional trends in higher education is the gradual overcoming of the particularity of institutions and the development of metropolitan universities which encompass areawide educational institutions and even some industries. Every aspect of education must receive careful scrutiny from the architecture of the dormitories to the nature of the grading system. These either add to or detract from the unique kind of educational experience that a college provides. Also the use of the most advanced technological teaching aids and inventions ought to be encouraged where they may be meaningfully related to the goals of the educational program.

Once I argued that the unique American synthesis in higher education involved taking the wrong element from both British and Continental universities.[61] From the ancient British universities we adopted the residential pattern for college education, but we abandoned the tutorial system as being too expensive and unsuited to the task of mass education. From the largely German model we adopted the lecture system but not the Continental indifference to student lodging and life. I once speculated that a more desirable synthesis would have been to avoid the expense of dormitory construction and place the money saved into increasing the number of teachers. Thus we might have been able to retain something approximating the tutorial system with its value of close association between professor and student.

I now believe that this alternative may also be undesirable. Students, by moving out of college dormitories at the earliest possible minute, are demonstrating that the sterile nature of much of dorm life is the most aggravating expression of *in loco parentis*. But in moving away from the campus, students tend to decrease their opportunities of contact with the faculty and with a broad cross section of their comrades. Dormitory life can be made a vital part of the educational experience if the dormitories include classrooms, living quarters for young faculty and their families, and even experiments such as the mixing of the sexes in the same residence. The American economy can make it possible for us to increase the amount of money spent on producing our most significant product—human beings. Not only can we afford more and better faculty, better physical plants, including more imaginatively designed dormitories, we cannot afford not to have them.

In simplest terms one might say that the overall goal and objective of higher education is that of making human life human. The college is the one place in society where all effort is or should be directed toward the communication, maintenance, and development of that *humanum* which is never simply given but always something achieved through great effort. This humanizing activity is carried on in part by establishing lines of communication with our cultural past but also by becoming aware of the dynamic present. It involves the creation, nurture, and sharpening of the critical intelligence. Karl Jaspers both posed the problem and stated the ideal when he wrote: "By its very name the university is a 'universe.' Discovery and research constitute an indivisible whole—departmentalization notwithstanding. The university deteriorates if it becomes an aggregate of specialized schools alongside of which it tolerates a so-called 'general education' as mere window dressing and vague talk in generalities. Scholarship depends on a relation to the whole. Individual disciplines are meaningless apart from their relation to the whole of knowledge. Therefore, it is the intention of a university to impart to its students a sense of the unity both of his own particular field of study and of all knowledge. The whole business of schooling, the mastery of routine and a body of facts, becomes harmful if it loses this sense of relatedness to the ideal of learning or actually prevents the student from living up to this ideal."[62]

Whether it likes it or not, the liberal arts college is today called upon to fulfill not only its traditional functions but those of the church, the family, and, to a lesser extent, of the state as well. It has become the locus of the discovery of meaning as well as a reform agent called upon to assist in the solution of the problems of a needy world. Never has society trusted educators to do so much as it does today.[63] The major question with which we are faced is whether the colleges and universities will accept these challenges and find the resources to meet these kinds of expectations. If the college is not to eschew or run away from these new responsibilities because of the magnitude of the tasks, it will need the understanding, good counsel, and genuine support of the other major institutions of society, particularly the state and the church. What is needed at the present crucial juncture is the coming together again of those coordinate centers of power, college, state, and church, which in the past created the most dynamic culture in human history to create a new synthesis to meet the demands of the future.

Notes

1. Johns Hopkins University pioneered in introducing to this country the Germanic pattern of higher education, particularly graduate education. Previously, the British model generally prevailed.

2. See the pamphlet "The Triple Revolution" (The Ad Hoc Committee on The Triple Revolution, Santa Barbara, Calif., 1964).

3. See Sherman S. Chickering, "How We Got That Way," *The American Scholar*, Autumn, 1967, pp. 602–607.

4. See W. David Maxwell, "A Methodological Hypothesis for the Plight of the Humanities," *Bulletin of the American Association of University Professors*, Vol. 54, No. 1 (March, 1968), pp. 78–84.

5. William Arrowsmith, "The Shame of the Graduate Schools," *Harper's Magazine*, March, 1966, pp. 51–59.

6. See comments in my book, *A Protestant Approach to the Campus Ministry* (The Westminster Press, 1964), pp. 73 ff.

7. "It is when the institution claims too much that it becomes suspect. And it is when an institution attempts to regulate beyond what is necessary to achieve its limited educational goals that it becomes vulnerable. Whether or not a student burns a draft card, participates in a civil rights march, engages in premarital or extra-marital sexual activity, becomes pregnant, attends church, sleeps all day, or drinks all night is not really the concern of a collegiate institution, as an educational institution. When colleges regulate such behavior, as many do, they are by implication taking responsibility for developing patriotism, one system of social standards, one system of health standards, and one religious stance—activities which more properly are the

province of other social institutions." Lewis B. Mayhew, "Changing the Balance of Power," *Saturday Review*, August 17, 1968, p. 58.

8. Martin Trow has delineated four student subcultures, the collegiate, the vocational, the academic, and the activist. "Student Cultures and Administrative Action," *Personality Factors on the College Campus* (University of Texas, Hogg Foundation for Mental Health, 1962).

9. Consider Ellul's comment: "To speak about crisis or chaos is to yield to an illusion. We are simply witnessing the disappearance of the old traditional forms to which we are accustomed—that is all. I say on the contrary that there isn't enough chaos. And my reason for saying this is precisely that man is incapable of controlling society's present forms—the organizing, systematizing forces." Jacques Ellul, "Between Chaos and Paralysis," *The Christian Century*, June 5, 1968, p. 747.

10. E.g., Marjorie Grene, *Introduction to Existentialism* (Phoenix, 1959); Eugene B. Borowitz, *A Layman's Introduction to Religious Existentialism* (The Westminster Press, 1965).

11. Mary Harrington Hall, "A Conversation with Michael Polanyi," *Psychology Today*, May, 1968.

12. See Thomas W. Ogletree (ed.), *Openings for Marxist-Christian Dialogue* (Abingdon Press, 1969).

13. See the article by Charles E. Wyzanski, Jr., chief judge of the U.S. District Court for Massachusetts, "A Federal Judge Digs the Young," *Saturday Review*, July 20, 1968.

14. Archibald MacLeish, "The Great American Frustration," *Saturday Review*, July 13, 1968, p. 16.

15. See Niebuhr's "The Two Sources of Western Culture," in *The Christian Idea of Education*, ed. by Edmund Fuller (Yale University Press, 1957), pp. 237–254.

16. Werner Heisenberg, *The Physicist's Conception of Nature* (London: Hutchinson, 1958), p. 29, quoted by Herbert Marcuse, *One-Dimensional Man* (Beacon Press, 1968), p. 152.

17. It has been observed that London had a smog problem as early as the thirteenth century because of the burning of soft coal. But not until the twentieth century does smog threaten the atmosphere of the whole earth.

18. Barry Commoner in an address, "Science and Survival," to the 23d National Conference on Higher Education, Chicago. I am much indebted to Dr. Commoner for insights and expressions that are reflected throughout this chapter.

19. Lynn White, Jr., states, "Since both our technological and our scientific movements got their start, acquired their character, and achieved world dominance in the middle ages, it would seem that we cannot understand their nature or their present impact upon ecology without examining fundamental medieval assumptions and developments." "The Historical Roots of Our Ecologic Crisis," *Science*, Vol. 155, No. 3767 (March 10, 1967), p. 1205.

20. "Our daily habits of action . . . are dominated by an implicit faith in perpetual progress which was unknown either to Greco-Roman antiquity or to the Orient. It is rooted in, and is indefensible apart from, Judeo-Christian theology. The fact that Communists share it merely helps to show what can be demonstrated on many other grounds: that Marxism, like Islam, is a Judeo-Christian heresy. We continue to live, as we have lived for about 1,700 years, very largely in a context of Christian axioms." *Ibid.*

21. See Tillich's essay, "The Idea and the Ideal of Personality," *The Protestant Era* (The University of Chicago Press, 1948), pp. 115–135.

22. Lynn White, Jr., *op. cit.*, pp. 1203–1207.

23. *Ibid.*, p. 1206.

24. George H. Williams, *Wilderness and Paradise in Christian Thought* (Harper & Row, Publishers, Inc., 1962).

25. For a brief but stimulating treatment of this process of westernization, see Arnold Toynbee, *The World and the West* (Oxford University Press, 1953).

26. See James Luther Adams, "The System of the Sci-

ences," *Paul Tillich's Philosophy of Culture, Science, and Religion* (Harper & Row Publishers, Inc., 1965), Ch. IV.

27. *Ibid.*, p. 126.

28. Herbert Marcuse, *One-Dimensional Man: Studies in the Ideology of Advanced Industrial Society* (Beacon Press, 1964, 5th printing, April, 1968).

29. Herbert Marcuse, *Reason and Revolution: Hegel and the Rise of Social Theory* (rev. ed., Oxford University Press; Beacon Press, 1960), p. 20.

30. Marcuse, *One-Dimensional Man*, p. 173. The result, Marcuse argues, was not only skepticism but conformism. The empiricist restriction of human nature to knowledge of the "given" removed the desire to transcend it.

31. *Ibid.* Cf. a work that has elicited much student interest, *Life Against Death* by Norman O. Brown (Random House, Inc., 1959).

32. Marcuse, *One-Dimensional Man*, p. 220.

33. *Ibid.*

34. A rehabilitated conception of what is meant by the term "reason" is badly needed in college classrooms.

35. Marcuse, *One-Dimensional Man*, p. 238.

36. Here Marcuse follows Kant and Tillich, Augustine.

37. Marcuse, *One-Dimensional Man*, p. 125.

38. The activist generation is right in accusing the older generation of hypocrisy, but it frequently lacks the ability to be aware of its own contradictions and shortcomings, e.g., they criticize the affluent for their materialism and at the same time for not making the same material goods available to minority groups. Many of the rebellious generation are content to be comfortably supported in their rebellion by "square" parents.

39. One of the humbling lessons that Western cultures are now in the process of learning is that they have something to learn from non-Western societies.

40. Williams, *op. cit.*, pp. 166–167.

41. It should be recalled that the medieval university was a much more open forum for the criticism of inherited

truth than seventeenth- and eighteen-century Counter Reformation and Protestant colleges and universities ever were.

42. This could be done by using monies contributed for individual student scholarships or by setting up impartial committees, broadly representative, such as those used within Britain to distribute the government grants.

43. Note the decline in the church school attendance, the leveling off of building programs, the scarcity of candidates for the ordained ministry, etc.

44. It is instructive to note that the American church has never been able to give rise to anything nearly as creative as the German Evangelical Academy.

45. The Jacob report in 1957 (*Changing Values in College*, by Philip E. Jacob. Harper & Brothers) and all subsequent studies confirm the importance of the co-curriculum and particularly the value of close student-faculty relationships in the acquisition and transformation of values.

46. Recall the bitter attack upon this phenomenon in Marcuse' *One-Dimensional Man.*

47. Some recommendations are given in the last chapter as to ways in which the colleges and universities may equip themselves to fulfill the challenges presented by the transfer to them of functions previously carried on by other institutions in society.

48. Adults are sometimes caught in the indefensible position of asking for political maturity from the students while refusing to let them have the political experience of governing themselves.

49. Studies of freshmen expectations will show how high they are. Study of them later in their college careers generally show how disappointed they have become in the failure of the colleges to fulfill these expectations.

50. John Wycliffe was master of Balliol College at Oxford; Hus was first a lecturer in philosophy at the University of Prague, then dean of the philosophy department, and finally rector of the University. Calvin and Erasmus both

had careers at and intimate connections with the University of Paris; Luther was a professor at the University of Wittenberg.

51. The Protestant Netherlands was the first to introduce higher education for women; and in Scotland, John Knox's unfulfilled educational scheme was the first comprehensive national educational system ever to be proposed.

52. One virtue of Ruedi Weber's schema is that it avoids the oversimplification of the traditional priestly versus prophetic tension. Scholarship has made us aware that the prophets were not as opposed to elements in the priestly tradition as was once supposed. But by terming the reformation theme the "Christ event theme," Ruedi Weber includes within the incarnational elements, grace, structure, renewal, as well as judgment and protest.

53. The conception of the world coming of age is, of course, not unique to Bonhoeffer. Nicolas Berdyaev used the expression and the conception can be traced back at least as far as Hegel.

54. Dietrich Bonhoeffer, *Prisoner for God* (The Macmillan Company, 1954), pp. 163–164.

55. Herein lies another advantage that the liberal arts college within a university possesses, potential access to graduate students and faculty. The unfortunate separation of most theological schools from major universities deprives theological students of many important aspects of modern professional education.

56. It is difficult, for example, to help students understand some of the apparently irrational allegiances and arguments of the brilliant minds of the past with respect, for example, to such conceptions as the divine right of kings, etc.

57. See the article "The View from the New Left," by Howard Zinn, professor of government at Boston University, *Vista*, Vol. 4, No. 1 (July–August, 1968), pp. 45–51.

58. Jeremy Larner, "Another Plane in Another Sphere: The College Drug Scene," in *The Troubled Campus* by eds. of the *Atlantic* (Atlantic Monthly Press, 1966), p. 23.

59. George R. Waggoner, "The Role of the Liberal Arts College," *Challenge and Change in American Education,* ed. by Seymour E. Harris, Kenneth Deitch, and Alan Levensohn (Berkeley, Calif.: McCutchan Publishing Corp., 1965), p. 285.

60. Prof. Daniel Bell makes an interesting case for this in a section of his work entitled "A Critique of Secondary School Reform," *Reforming of General Education,* Columbia University Press, 1966), p. 139.

61. John E. Cantelon, *op. cit.,* pp. 115–116.

62. Karl Jaspers, *The Ideal of the University* (Beacon Press, 1959), p. 46.

63. An example may be seen in the setting up of a Presidential committee to study violence. Much of the research component will be farmed out to colleges and universities.